BRANDO

By the Same Authors

LANA: The Public and Private Lives of Miss Turner
JUDY: The Films and Career of Judy Garland
REBELS: The Rebel Hero in Films
THOSE GREAT MOVIE ADS
with Eleanor Clark

BRANDO

The Unauthorized Biography

JOE MORELLA
and
EDWARD Z. EPSTEIN

Crown Publishers, Inc., New York

To our families
★ *and our great friend Maddy Solter* ★

The authors gratefully acknowledge the cooperation of individuals who granted interviews in connection with this book.

Also, special thanks to James Bonavita, Patrick B. Clark, David C. L'Heureux, John Madden, Jim Pearsall, Geoffrey Wheatley, and Madeline Jones Solter.

THE STORY goes that when Marlon Brando first became a major star and trekked to Hollywood, his agents and press agents, anxious to please, made it clear they could and would satisfy his every desire. He had only to name it. Brando thought this over during the limousine ride with his agents from the airport to the hotel. Concerned about an unhappy, particularly nervous pet monkey he was traveling with, Brando finally replied: "Okay. Get my monkey fucked."

A sense of humor—variously described as playful, childlike, exasperating and/or sadistic—and gift for the absurd. Along with an incredible talent for acting, these are standard Marlon Brando equipment.

"Expect the unexpected from him and you'll get along fine," advises an ex-business associate. "He's basically discontented with himself and his life. This can create a lot of chaos. But once you accept his ground rules he's a pussycat."

The pussycat will pass the half-century mark on April 3, 1974. "Fifty going on a hundred and fifty. He's squeezed a lot of life into that half century," notes a friend. The highlights: superstardom for two generations, despite a succession of flop films that would have finished off any other actor; a public private life that has included trouble-haunted marriages and divorces—this despite his efforts to keep his personal life private. There have been illegitimate children; countless lawsuits; a paternity suit; suicide attempts by former girl friends; child custody battles; psychoanalysis; involvements in social causes for which he has sometimes received censure, not praise, even from the groups he has tried to help.

The years of hard living haven't slipped by unnoticed. Once the ultimate male sex symbol, brooding, beautiful, violent, and gentle simultaneously, the prototype for ensuing generations of actors, Brando today is paunchy, balding, unmistakably middle-aged.

Thousands of women have dreamt of bedding down with Marlon Brando. What would it be like? There are conflicting reports. He's gentle, sensitive, and loving, say some. However, according to the former Mrs. Brando, Anna Kashfi, "As a romancer, Marlon leaves a lot to be desired. He's just plain clumsy and that's the truth. If he were not a film star I doubt whether he'd get to first base with women." Jet-set darling Bianca Jagger, wife of Rolling Stone Mick Jagger, was also one of Brando's conquests. She remembers him with even less kind remarks than Miss Kashfi.

But, in the words of a recent lover: "He's more than a man. He's an experience."

At this midpoint in his life, Marlon Brando has a multitude of experiences to look back upon.

Unlike many legendary show-business figures, his background isn't from a humble, suffer-in-a-garret or work-four-shows-a-day-in-vaudeville scenario. Nor was he plagued by parents anxious to exploit him. On the contrary. "My father was indifferent to me," Brando admitted as an adult. "Nothing I could do interested him or pleased him."

Marlon Sr. was a prosperous salesman-manufacturer of limestone products in the early 1920s. The Brando forebears were French and spelled the name Brandeau. Brando's lovely wife, Dorothy Pennebaker, a tall, attractive woman nicknamed Dodie, had given birth to two daughters, Frances and Jocelyn, before the arrival of first son Marlon in Omaha, Nebraska, on April 3, 1924.

Dodie Brando was and always had been stagestruck.

8

She was a sensitive, gentle but strong-spirited woman. Dedicated to Theatre she lived in towns that had no Theatre to speak of and worked hard to remedy that situation. She was on the board of directors of the local Omaha Community Playhouse and acted in its productions. It was "Doe" Brando who gave gangling young Omaha teenager Henry Fonda his first taste of theatre in an early Playhouse production.

"Dodie *loved* the theatre," remembers a contemporary. "She was happiest when doing something in or connected with it." Her enthusiasm for the arts, for creative people, was a dominant force of Brando homelife. She passed this love of living a creative life on to her three children. And they worshipped her.

"Marlon's mother was a very fine actress," Brando Sr. recalled. "She never did anything with it but nevertheless she created an interest in acting in the three children."

Though her husband tolerated her devotion to a world of fantasy, according to a contemporary he considered theatre, actors, the whole business, a waste of time and definitely not a profession for his son. Years later Brando Sr. contradicted this. "I was never against the kids doing anything as long as they did it well."

On occasion Brando and his wife would argue, sometimes heatedly. Because children view the world in the light of their home experience, young Marlon would never forget the agony of his mother's unhappiness. She was unable to cope with her frustrations as an actress and took refuge in the bottle. Many years later Marlon revealed the painful truth. "My mother was everything to me. A whole world. I tried so hard. I used to come home from school. There wouldn't be anybody home. Nothing in the icebox. Then the telephone would ring. Somebody calling from some bar. And they'd say, 'We've got a lady down here. You'd better come get her.'"

Writer Maurice Zolotow, commenting on Brando's growing up under "petticoat influence," commented, "She made it almost impossible for him to develop a sense of security about being a man. All his life Brando oscillated between the polar

9

attractions of his parents and has had a difficult time finding out what he, himself, is."

While it was inaccurately reported years later that Marlon Jr., or Bud as he was then called, loved to "delight" his family with a never-ending supply of "antics," in actuality "he drove them nuts during those years," remembers a friend. "It was a matter of seeing how much he could get away with." For instance, how long could he hold his breath? How fast could he eat? He was particularly expert at pretending to fall down dead. "Even as a youngster, always giving performances," recollects an old neighbor.

When Bud was six, the family moved to Evanston, Illinois, then to California, and a short time later back to Illinois, this time to Libertyville. It was a rural town and the Brandos settled in a rambling house in a country neighborhood. They kept chickens, rabbits, geese, had a horse, cow, a Great Dane, and twenty-eight cats. Supposedly one of Bud's daily chores was milking the cow.

The boy was constantly bringing home injured animals to be healed. Once he kept unearthing a dead chicken which his mother had to repeatedly rebury. On one occasion he brought home a woman he met on the street, telling his mother that she was sick and needed a place to stay. Mrs. Brando made suitable arrangements for the woman.

Brando Jr. was always drawn to the underdog. In the opinion of an old school chum, "I always thought that was because he could feel superior, or at least not inferior. Bud was looked up to by these people." Bud's grandmother, years later, remarked that he "always brought home cross-eyed girls."

Bud was competitive. Extroverted. "I liked athletics . . . track and football. And I liked the music appreciation course and some of the science courses. But I was always much more interested in reading geographical magazines than in studying."

He hated being told what to do and when to do it. Consequently it was no surprise that he loathed school. His dislike for it manifested itself in ways that didn't meet with the approval of his teachers.

Brando did poorly at Libertyville Township High School. According to its then principal, H. E. Underbrink, "Brando was rather irresponsible. He wasn't interested in anything in particular. His record was poor. He rarely took part in any extracurricular activities because practically every afternoon he was in our 3:15 P.M. disciplinary period."

Out of desperation Bud's father finally sent him to military school, the Shattuck Academy in Minnesota, which Brando Sr. had attended. Bud, anxious to please his dad, started off rather well, even landing roles in two of the school's productions. But his father's continued attitude of general indifference had its impact on his son's attitude toward—and future with—the school.

Around about this time Bud and his mother visited California. Doe looked up her old friend and protégé Henry Fonda, who was by now a leading Hollywood star. Brando's aunt contends that fifteen-year-old Marlon was seriously attracted to the idea of acting after meeting and spending time with Fonda.

Back at the Shattuck Academy, Bud's behavior led to difficulties. A few weeks before graduation he was expelled. According to one source he was caught smoking. Another source claims the reason was the school director's lack of sense of humor when Marlon emptied a chamberpot out the window without first checking to see if anyone was walking beneath. Also, according to Brando, "I made a bomb of firecrackers and placed it against one teacher's door. Then I poured a trail of hair tonic from the bomb to my room, and set fire to it. I figured the flame would burn the alcohol away, leaving no evidence to spoil my alibi that I had been studying in my room. The hair tonic fuse worked all right, but it left a trail of scorched flooring to my door. I was expelled."

Years later Brando referred to the school as "the asylum." "I hated it every day I was there," he said. "The authorities annoyed me. I had to show respect to those for whom I had no respect. I also hated clocks. I love the kind of life where time doesn't matter, but the bell at the academy chimed every quarter hour and I loathed it because it reminded me of things I had to do. One night I climbed to the top of the tower and worked the clapper loose. Then I buried it in the ground." The authorities, unable to replace the bell, posted cadets around the academy grounds who blew their bugles every quarter hour. Poor Marlon: "Those buglers were worse than the bell."

He never finished school. However, in later years his thirst for knowledge and self-improvement literally knew no bounds.

Then as now Brando was searching for something to believe in. At seventeen he decided he wanted to become a minister. An intimate relates, "He needs to find something in life—something in himself—that is permanently true, and he needs to lay down his life for it. For such an intense personality, nothing less than that will do." However, Bud was talked out of following the ministry as a career.

After expulsion from school, Brando worked as a tile contractor. "The idea of strenuous open-air work seemed attractive and grown-up." He described the job: "We had to drain farmland with a huge machine and lay tile in the ditches the machine dug. The job was dull and dirty, but I stuck it out for six weeks. Then I quit."

He trekked to New York in the fall of 1943. His sister Frances was studying painting there at the Art Students League. It was the height of World War II. "I was 4-F," noted Marlon. A trick knee was the cause. "My father told me I had to find a job. I had to do something."

In New York the nineteen-year-old drifted through a series of odd jobs, working for several days as an elevator operator at Best and Company, the Fifth Avenue department store, beating drums at a joint called The Cockatoo Club, driving a truck, and selling lemonade.

He lived with his sister Frances for a while. Later he moved to out-of-the-way cold-water flats or, subsequently, sublet apartments of friends. On one occasion it was a two-room attic

apartment in the Murray Hill section. Another time it was an apartment shared with Wally Cox, a lifelong friend.

Whatever the place it never seemed to be a permanent home in the eyes of those who viewed it. Brando's only possessions were a tomtom, a recorder, a small red piano, and whatever books he happened to be reading at the moment. His "wardrobe": T-shirts and blue jeans. He owned a suit, but when he wore it it was usually with a T-shirt.

It was inevitable that Marlon would enroll at acting school. In the words of an old friend, "Doe Brando's obsession with the theatre had its impact on her son. Marlon's father's hopes for a business career for his boy—or some kind of career with a reliable future—were in vain."

According to Marlon, choosing a career in acting was "really only chance. My sister Jocelyn was already acting and I thought I'd give it a whirl too."

The Dramatic Workshop of the New School for Social Research was a leading acting school of the day.

Marlon enrolled there. He was developing into "a very sexy young man. He was the most desirable, sensual young guy I ever saw," remembers an actress who has since retired from the profession to become the wife of an important motion picture executive. "My God, he had animal magnetism that grabbed you. And a beautiful, sensitive face. He could be a charmer when he wanted to. He had *it* and we all knew it."

"In my opinion," states a friend from that era, "there were always two Marlons fighting for supremacy. The 'animal' and the poet. Not quite split like Jekyll and Hyde but there nonetheless. They're still fighting, I think."

He appeared in several student productions under the direction of Erwin Piscator. In a performance of Gerhart Hauptmann's *Hannele's Way to Heaven*, Marlon played two parts—the schoolteacher and an angel in the dream sequence. Critic George Freedley wrote that Marlon gave the best performance.

He continued to gain acting experience in classical

works. While at the New School he also appeared in Shakespeare's *Twelfth Night* and adaptations of several Molière plays. Freedley caught the *Twelfth Night* performance: "Marlon Brando handled the tiny bit of Sebastian satisfactorily though it would have been interesting to have seen what he might have done with Feste or Orsino."

Marlon decided to study under famed acting coach Stella Adler. Talented, flamboyant, volatile, intense, and dedicated, she is described by an associate as "a genius and a character."

Stella, sister of actor Luther Adler and then wife of director-producer Harold Clurman, was at least twenty years older than Marlon. Many feel that she is responsible for Brando's occasional attraction to older women.

"Stella was Mother Earth to her students," recalls an observer. "Marlon was enthralled with her. She captured his imagination. She taught him acting technique."

"I taught him nothing," said Stella many years later. "I opened up possibilities of thinking, feeling, experiencing, and as I opened those doors, he walked right through. He never needed me after that. . . . He lives the life of the actor twenty-four hours a day. If he is talking to you, he will absorb everything about you—your smile, the way your teeth grow. His style is the perfect marriage of intuition and intelligence."

Brando courted Stella Adler's attractive young daughter, Ellen. Few people are aware that it was a relationship that lasted many years, with Ellen "waiting patiently" (and in vain) for him to settle down. This was one of the first of many similar relationships Brando would engage in with "special" women in his life.

Stella Adler predicted that Marlon Brando would, within a year, be "the best young actor in the American theatre."

During the summer of '44 he again acted under Piscator's direction, this time with a stock company in Sayville, Long Island. He was fired but on the same day was signed for his first Broadway role. In the fall, at the age of twenty, Marlon Brando made his Broadway debut. He played the part of fifteen-year-old Nels in *I Remember Mama.* Critical comment about him was favorable but hardly of the *A Star Is Born* variety.

For the show's Playbill, Brando provided himself with an elaborate and highly fanciful biographical sketch, claiming he was born in Calcutta where his father was doing geological research and the family came to the U.S. when Marlon was six months old. In other programs he listed his birthplace as Bangkok, Bombay, Mindanao, and Rangoon. "Why shouldn't I have a different place for my birth in each theatre program if I feel like it?" observed Brando years later. "What difference does it make where you're born? It's such a curious thing to talk about. It's the same thing as talking about whether I ever ate a meal of gazelle eyes or not. I told one writer I'd done that, but I was kidding. He took me seriously and printed it as the truth."

During his years in New York, Marlon also took courses at the New School in psychology, the history of art, conversational French, and graphology. He always seemed to be reading what his friends described as "deep stuff."

Brando's offstage behavior caused comment from the beginning. Stories were told of his playing drums so loud into the early hours of the morning that the police had to be called. Of holding a raw egg in his hand when an important Hollywood executive wanted to shake it. Of carrying a Yo-Yo with him to his first screen test in 1944. (He failed the test.) Of eating raw eggs for breakfast. Of hating to answer telephones and letting them ring as much as twenty times. Of using impersonations of different people when he finally did answer. Of crying when he read *Bambi* and saw *The Wizard of Oz.*

There's the tale of young Brando telling off Broadway's living legends Alfred Lunt and Lynn Fontanne. This occurred when he went to audition for a Lunt-Fontanne production and was handed a script and told to read certain lines on a certain page. Brando, not used to this type of approach, hesitated. The Lunts, apparently sensing his difficulty, told him to say anything he wished. He said "Hickory, dickory, dock" and walked out.

According to the Lunts, this *O Mistress Mine* audition was less dramatic. "He walked across the stage for us," recalled Alfred Lunt. "He looked too old for the part. He looked at least 22 . . . it was important that the boy be around 16 years old or at least look 16 . . . Marlon Brando was polite and thanked us for hearing him. I have heard this hickory-dickory-dock story many times and I imagine that when he became famous, Brando decided to make a character for himself, and rudeness was part of this character . . . But I must tell you in all honesty that he was not in the least rude to us."

For some time Brando didn't appear in stage productions although he continued to study acting. It was another pattern he would follow, taking time off to travel or "be by himself." (Later, after Brando became a superstar, his recluselike habits caused many in the business who resented his "quick success" to spread a flock of absurd rumors regarding Marlon's early New York days. One of the most ridiculous said that he had been a $100-a-night "callboy" and that his picture was in a special "catalog" sent to an elite clientele interested in such expensive diversions.)

He began studying with actor-turned-director Elia Kazan. On one occasion, under Kazan's guidance, he directed a student production of *Hedda Gabler*.

Early in 1946 Brando was back on Broadway, this time in the role of Sarge McRae, a war veteran who murders his faithless wife, in Maxwell Anderson's *Truckline Cafe*. It was an ill-fated play but provided Brando with good notices. The public exhibited interest in him. And so did Broadway's glamorous but aging leading ladies of the day.

Brando portrayed Marchbanks to Katharine Cornell's Candida for the revival of the Shaw classic, directed by Guthrie McClintic. Some reports state it was McClintic who wanted Brando for the role, others claim Cornell insisted on the virile young actor as her costar.

Marlon's reviews were mixed. "It was really not his kind

of role," says a friend. "And Cornell was simply not his ideal leading lady."

From *Candida,* Brando went into Ben Hecht's *A Flag Is Born,* which was about the new country, Israel. He played David, a refugee Jew. Critics now called him "a bright new star." His next play—or confrontation, as some friends described it—was *The Eagle Has Two Heads*. The star was formidable, unshy Tallulah Bankhead.

Tallulah and Marlon "didn't get along."

"He drove me to distraction picking his nose, pausing too long and scratching himself," bellowed Tallulah. Brando "left" the play. Regarding their personality clash, in later years Brando simply said, "She didn't like me." Others said that Tallulah had indeed liked "the young Adonis," although he was an upstart, and wanted him to become her lover. When he wouldn't she was furious and had him fired. (Looking back at *The Eagle Has Two Heads* after he was a star, Brando summed up the experience by crossing himself, grinning: "Then came Tallulah!")

Marlon took another year-long respite. He spent his time thinking, brooding, traveling abroad and not worrying about his career.

"I FIRST MET HIM IN 1947, when I was casting 'Streetcar.' I had very little money at the time and was living simply in a broken-down house near Provincetown. I had a houseful of people, the plumbing was flooded and someone had blown the light fuse. Someone said a kid named Brando was down on the beach and looked good. He arrived at dusk, wearing Levi's, took one look at the confusion around him, and set to work. First he stuck his hand into the overflowing toilet bowl and unclogged the drain, then he tackled the fuses. Within an hour, everything worked. You'd think he had spent his entire antecedent life repairing drains. Then he read the script aloud, just as he played it. It was the most magnificent reading I ever heard and he had the part immediately. He stayed the night, slept curled up with an old quilt in the center of the floor."

This was Tennessee Williams's first encounter with Marlon Brando.

Brando was again studying with Kazan, who had sent him up to Provincetown to meet Williams. The director had always recognized Marlon's potential as a great actor but knew the boy had deep-seated problems which had to be overcome before he could realize that potential. Kazan sent him to his own analyst, Dr. Bela Mittelmann.

Despite Tennessee Williams's statement that Brando "had the part immediately" in *Streetcar,* he hadn't.

In 1947, John Garfield was at the height of his career. He was free of his Warner Brothers contract and had produced and starred in his greatest success, *Body and Soul,* for which he received an Oscar nomination. Garfield had come from the New York stage and at this point in his life wanted to return to it. He was offered the lead in the new play by Tennessee Williams, *A Streetcar Named Desire.*

Williams was already an acknowledged genius, having scored an enormous success with *The Glass Menagerie* a couple of seasons earlier. His new play concerned a tragic southern belle brutalized by life and dealt the final blow by her cruel, badgering, animalistic Polish-American brother-in-law, Stanley Kowalski.

The role of Blanche Du Bois was one Williams had written and developed several times before in one-act plays.

Garfield turned down the part of Kowalski, feeling that the role of Blanche overshadowed it. Williams and Kazan then agreed that twenty-three-year-old Marlon Brando was the man for the part.

Brando was exceptionally good-looking in those days, seemingly too "pretty" for Kowalski. But he possessed the necessary animal magnetism and physical strength to play the part. Established stage star Jessica Tandy won the role of Blanche.

Truman Capote has recalled meeting Marlon at a rehearsal of the play. "It was a winter afternoon in New York . . . he was still relatively unknown; at least, I hadn't a clue to who he might be when, arriving too early at the 'Streetcar' rehearsal, I found the auditorium deserted and a brawny young man stretched out atop a table on the stage under the gloomy glare of work lights, solidly asleep. Because he was wearing a white T shirt and denim trousers, because of his squat gymnasium physique—the weight-lifter's arms, the Charles Atlas chest though an opened 'Basic Writings of Sigmund Freud' was resting on it—I took him for a stagehand. Or did until I looked closely at his face. It was as if a stranger's head had been attached to the brawny body, as in certain counterfeit photographs. For this face was so very untough, superimposing, as it did, an almost angelic refinement and gentleness upon hard-jawed good looks: taut skin, a broad, high forehead, wide-apart eyes, an aquiline nose, full lips with a relaxed, sensual expression. Not the least suggestion of Williams' unpoetic Kowalski. It was therefore rather an experience to observe, later that afternoon, with what chameleon ease Brando acquired the character's cruel and gaudy colors, how superbly, like a guileful salamander, he slithered into the part, how his own persona evaporated. . . ."

Streetcar was a major project for all concerned. On December 3, 1947, Broadway, as it had done and would continue to do on selective occasions, witnessed the birth of a star. Brando was electrifying. He introduced a character not seen in New York theatre before, a character born out of Sandburg's "Chicago" and the sweatshops of early America, out of Whitman's *Leaves of Grass* and the slums of immigrants. In the words of a director who was there: "It was awful and it was sublime. Only once in a generation do you see such a thing in the theatre."

Brando viewed Kowalski as "aggressive, unpremeditated, overt and completely without doubt about himself." His acting was a tremendous achievement since the character was exactly the opposite of real-life Marlon who was, in the opinion of Kazan, "possibly the gentlest person I have ever known."

Brando's parents came to New York for opening night. It was the first time Marlon's friends had ever seen them. An observer remembered, "Marlon always gave a very colorful picture of homelife back in Illinois. When we heard that his family was coming to New York for the opening of 'Streetcar' everybody was very curious. We didn't know what to expect. On opening night producer Irene Selznick gave a big party at '21.' Marlon came with his mother and father. Well, you can't imagine two more attractive people. Tall, handsome, charming as they could be. What impressed me—I think it amazed everyone—was Marlon's attitude toward them. In their presence, he wasn't the lad we knew. He was a model son. Reticent, respectful, very polite, considerate in every way."

However, on many occasions Jessica Tandy had to endure the "other" Marlon. "Offstage he drove Jessica nuts with his

Marlon Brando's parents: Marlon Brando Sr. and Dorothy Pennebaker Brando

bongo playing," remembers a friend. Marlon insulted columnist Sheilah Graham, when, introduced to her by Miss Tandy, he turned to Jessica and said: "Is this your mother?" He created additional problems for Tandy the Actress. His pranks often ruined her best scenes. One night, when she was in the throes of a dramatic speech, she noticed the audience was restless and some people were even giggling when they should have been absorbed in the drama. She looked around and saw that Brando, stone-faced, had shoved a cigarette up one of his nostrils.

During these and ensuing years Marlon's reputation as "a loner" began taking shape. A friend recalls, "He was a brooder all right. He seemed to have a built-in hideway room and was always running off to it to worry over himself, and gloat, too, like a miser with his gold. But it wasn't all gloomsville. When he wanted to, he could rocket right out of himself. He had a wild, kid kind of fun thing. Once, he was living in an old brownstone on 52nd Street, near where some of the jazz joints were. He used to go up on the roof and fill paper bags with water and throw them down at the stiffs coming out of the clubs. He had a sign on the wall of his room that said, 'You Ain't Livin If You Don't Know It.' He could be sweet. He was the least opportunistic person I've ever known. He never gave a damn about anybody who could help him; you might say he went out of his way to avoid them. Sure, part of that—the kind of people he didn't like and the kind he did, both—stemmed from his insecurities, his inferiority feelings. Very few of his friends were his equals—anybody he'd have to *compete* with, if you know what I mean. Mostly they were strays, idolizers, characters who were dependent on him one way or another. The same with the girls he took out. Plain sort of somebody's-secretary-type girls—nice enough but nothing that's going to start a stampede of competitors."

An amusing anecdote concerns Brando and roommate Wally Cox when they lived in the brownstone on Fifty-second Street. Their apartment was near the now extinct restaurant Leon & Eddie's, and they annoyed the management by parking their motorcycles in front of the restaurant.

Brando at play at one of his favorite early pastimes

The story goes that one night Brando and Cox were refused admittance to the restaurant because of Brando's attire (T-shirt and jeans). The irate Brando took a bucket, went to Central Park, and filled it with horse manure. From his apartment he hurled the contents of the bucket in the direction of Leon & Eddie's, shouting, "Watch out for the Flying Red Horse!" (He was referring to the then popular trademark of the Socony Oil Company.)

These were Marlon's "fun" years in New York. Regarding his way of life then: "It's as though Marlon lived in a house where the doors are never locked," remembered a friend. "When he lived in New York, the door always *was* open. Anybody could come in, whether Marlon was there or not, and everybody did. You'd arrive and there would be ten, fifteen characters wandering around. It was strange, because nobody seemed to really know anybody else. They were just there, like people in a bus station. Some type asleep in a chair. People reading the tabs. A girl dancing by herself. Or painting her toenails. A comedian trying out his nightclub act. Off in a corner, there'd be a chess game going. And drums—bang, boom, bang, boom! But there was never any drinking—nothing like that. Once in a while, somebody would say, 'Let's go down to the corner for an ice-cream soda.' Now, in all this Marlon was the common denominator, the only connecting link. He'd move around the room drawing individuals aside and talking to them alone. If you've noticed, Marlon can't, *won't,* talk to two people simultaneously. He'll never take part in a *group* conversation. It always has to be a cozy tête-à-tête— one person at a time. Which is necessary, I suppose, if you use the same kind of charm on everyone. But even when you know that's what he's doing, it doesn't matter. Because when *your* turn comes, he makes you feel you're the only person in the room. In the world. Makes you feel that you're under his protection and that your troubles and moods concern him deeply. You have to believe it; more than anyone I've known, he radiates *sincerity*. Afterward, you may ask yourself, 'Is it an act?' If so, what's the point? What have you got to give him? Nothing except—and this *is* the point—affection. Affection that lends him authority over you. I sometimes think Marlon is like an orphan who later on in life tries to compensate by becoming the kindly head of a huge orphanage. But even outside this institution he wants everybody to love him."

During the run of *Streetcar* Brando broke his nose. It changed his looks considerably. "I did it boxing. . . . We, some of the guys backstage and me—we used to go down to the boiler room in the theatre and horse around, mix it up. One night, I was mixing it up with this guy and—crack! So I put on my coat and walked around to the nearest hospital—it was off Broadway somewhere. My nose was really busted. They had to give me an anesthetic to set it, and put me to bed. Not that I was sorry. 'Streetcar' had been running about a year and I was sick of it. But my nose healed pretty quick, and I guess I would've been back in the show practically right away if I hadn't done what I did to Irene Selznick." Mrs. Selznick, daughter of MGM movie mogul Louis B. Mayer and first wife of producer David O. Selznick, was the producer of *Streetcar*. "There is one shrewd lady," remembered Brando. "When she wants something, she wants it. And she wanted me back in the play. But when I heard she was coming to the hospital, I went to work with bandages and iodine and mercurochrome, and—Christ!—when she walked in the door, I looked like my head had been cut off. At the least. And *sounded* as though I were dying. 'Oh, Marlon,' she said, 'you poor, *poor* boy!' And I said, 'Don't you worry about anything, Irene. I'll be back in the show tonight!' And she said, 'Don't you dare! We can manage without you for—for—well, a *few* days more.' 'No, no,' I said. 'I'm O.K. I want to work. Tell them I'll be back tonight.' So she said, 'You're in no condition, you poor darling. I *forbid* you to come to the theatre.' So I stayed in the hospital and had myself a ball."

Mrs. Selznick later remarked, "They didn't set his nose properly at all. Suddenly his face was quite different. Kind of tough. For months afterward, I kept telling him, 'But they've *ruined* your face. You must have your nose broken again and reset.' Luckily for him, he didn't listen to me. Because I honestly think that broken nose made his fortune as far as the movies go. It gave him sex appeal. He was too beautiful before."

It was during these years that his "special" relationship with his beloved mother was shattered forever. . . . "My mother. She broke apart like a piece of porcelain." When he was eighteen he had thought ". . . if she loved me enough, trusted me enough, I thought, then we can be together, in New York; we'll live together and I'll take care of her." Later on, that really happened. "She left my father and came to live with me. . . . I tried so hard. But my love wasn't enough. She couldn't care enough. She went back. And one day—I didn't care anymore. She was there. In a room. Holding on to me. And I let her fall. Because I couldn't take it any more—watch her breaking apart, in front of me, like a piece of porcelain. I stepped right over her. I walked right out. I was indifferent. Since then, I've been indifferent."

In 1948, Jocelyn Brando, who had changed her name to Jocelyn Hammer then back to Brando, was playing the nurse in *Mister Roberts*, which starred old family friend Henry Fonda. Jocelyn got raves for her performance.

The Brandos were riding high, professionally. *Streetcar* won the Pulitzer Prize and Drama Critic's Circle Award. Marlon's income was $550 weekly, but money never seemed to stay long in his possession. He telephoned his father. "Pop, I can't handle this money situation. Can you do something about it?" His father later noted, "All his life I knew Marlon never cared anything about money. It's never been important to him so I figured somebody had to help him and I agreed."

From then on $400 of Marlon's weekly salary was sent home for Brando Sr. to invest. However, Jr. still couldn't hold onto the remaining $150 a week. He observed at the time, "I don't buy clothes, I don't go to nightclubs, I don't drink, I eat in cafeterias, I haven't got a car, I've never paid more than $65 a month rent—but I've never got any money."

What he didn't say was that he was a soft touch, easily

giving out "loans," which were never paid back. Friends saw him plunk down a twenty dollar bill for a cup of coffee, not bothering about the change. Brando was unconcerned. "I haven't made up my mind about money. I haven't decided what it *means*."

Marlon, so completely introspective, was still a deeply troubled man. His traumatic experiences with his mother had taken their toll. He was deep in psychoanalysis. "It was my misery that made me go," he stated candidly, "misery long enough and strong enough to force my getting assistance in solving my difficulties. I was suffering from headaches that lasted as long as four days.

"People are usually willing to blame somebody else before they blame themselves. I was the same way. But I had enough good sense to realize that if I wanted well-being, psycho-analytic therapy was just about the only, and last, way I could get it."

In 1948 a young ad agency man, Bob Condon, was at a party and found himself seated next to a young man he has described as "a rather non-descript chap dressed in blue jeans and a turtle neck shirt. He had compelling eyes and a sort of sneer that encompassed the whole room." Condon introduced himself and the young man replied, "I'm Martin Bumby." Condon subsequently saw pictures of Bumby in the papers and read complaints from theatre critics about his diction and realized that he had thought he heard the name Bumby when Brando had said Brando.

They became friends and were in fact neighbors on Fifty-second Street. "Marlon had the run of my place whenever he wanted it," Condon has remembered. "For instance, he developed a liking for fresh orange juice but had no squeezer in his room. Being an early riser and not wanting to disturb me, he would go through the fire door onto the terrace and climb through the kitchen window. Then he would carefully and quietly remove two oranges from a paper bag, cut them, squeeze them, drink the juice and just as quietly clean up and steal away out the window and into the dawn. Several times overnight guests would scream as the window slid open and then stare open-mouthed as Stanley Kowalski crept over the sill."

Brando and Condon sometimes visited the Central Park Zoo on weekends. On one such occasion they visited the primate house. The keeper warned them not to go near the big baboon's cage because the ape sometimes spat in people's faces. Marlon wasn't worried since, as he explained to Condon, animals got "friendly vibrations" from him. Condon recalled ensuing events. "He stepped right up to the railing and smiled at the glowering beast. Mr. Baboon spit and hit Marlon square in the face." Marlon went to a drinking fountain, wiped his face, filled his mouth with water "and came back and gave the ape 'whatfor' in exactly the same way." The baboon was horrified and ran to the back of his cage. The keeper was furious but Marlon, "cool and inscrutable, said, 'If more people did that it would teach that damn ape some manners.'"

As he was nearing completion of his run in *Streetcar*, Brando declared: "I want to travel. I want to go to Rangoon and Bangkok. I want to go to Paris. I want to act in French movies, where you can show *life*, identification with real people. In French pictures you can live, make love, do everything that people *really* do."

How did twenty-four-year-old Marlon react to Success? "It took me a long time before I was aware that that's what I was —a big success. I was so absorbed in myself, my own problems, I never looked around, took account. I used to walk in New York, miles and miles, walk in the streets late at night, and never *see* anything. I was never sure about acting, whether that was what I really wanted to do; I'm still not. Then, when I was in 'Streetcar' and it had been running a couple of months, one night— dimly, dimly—I began to hear this roar. It was like I'd been asleep, and I woke up here sitting on a pile of candy."

Years later Brando claimed that analysis had been a big help to him. "I don't say I've found happiness, but I've certainly lost chronic misery. Happiness comes to you from time to time; it isn't something that you put on like a hat and wear forever.

But I'm considerably less restless—less at odds with things. I've also lost my kind of zest for traveling—or running away. I don't feel obligated to go tearing off at a moment's notice to India or Bangkok."

He also candidly stated, "I was afraid of analysis at first. Afraid it might destroy the impulses that made me creative, an artist. A sensitive person receives fifty impressions where somebody else may only get seven. Sensitive people are so vulnerable; they're so easily brutalized and hurt just because they *are* sensitive. The more sensitive you are, the more certain you are to be brutalized, develop scabs. Never evolve. Never allow yourself to feel anything, because you always feel too much. Analysis helps. It helped me."

$\star$ *3* $\star$

"SIGN BRANDO."

It was obvious even to the dumbest nephews of the reigning movie moguls that after his Broadway triumph in *Streetcar* Marlon Brando would be the next matinee idol. However, film people weren't prepared for this new breed of actor who, like Montgomery Clift, another "hot" property of the day, expressed contempt for Hollywood and ignored film offers.

"They've never made an honest picture in their lives, and probably never will," observed young Marlon.

"He was always full of shit," declares a cynical movie executive who was in on negotiations for Brando's first film deals. "He was just a shrewd character who knew how to drive a hard bargain. He signed, didn't he? Okay, he didn't go for a long-term deal but he had good advice. He gambled that he would click and could double and triple his price right away."

Before going to Hollywood Marlon took a trip to Paris, a city he has always loved. He has gone there often and had, on his first visit, realized a longtime ambition. He met the one film actress he admired above all others. She had starred in the classic *Children of Paradise,* which Marlon once described as "Maybe the best movie ever made. You know, that's the only time I ever fell in love with an actress, somebody on the screen. I was mad about Arletty. I mean I was really in *love* with her. My first trip to Paris, the thing I did right away, I asked to meet Arletty. I went to see her as though I were going to a shrine. My ideal woman. . . .

Wow! Was that a mistake, was that a disillusionment. She was a tough article."

After the European jaunt, Marlon headed for Hollywood. Producer Stanley Kramer, noted for commercial films on controversial subjects, lured him with a challenging Carl Foreman script (*The Men*) and a guarantee that Fred Zinnemann would direct. Brando's salary for the picture would be $40,000. No long-term contracts were involved in the strictly one-picture deal.

Brando had initially turned down Kramer's offer, despite the producer's pleas via transatlantic telephone. But then, in Brando's words: "My agent forwarded me a seven or eight page synopsis of the story with some of the dialogue and I read it one day walking down the street. It had what I felt was an important dramatic situation. Take this guy and his girl, the guy completely helpless, worse than a baby or an animal. It's impossible to realize such terrible frustration and hopelessness unless you live like that."

The Men was a semidocumentary-style film about paraplegics at the Birmingham Veterans Administration Hospital near Hollywood. The plot concerned the love affair between Brando, a victim of World War II unwilling to be rehabilitated, and his fiancée, portrayed by Teresa Wright.

Brando set the tone of his Hollywood stay with his first comments: "The only reason I'm here is because I don't yet have the moral strength to turn down the money." He arrived in the clothes-conscious glamour town wearing a suit with a hole in it and slits in the seams. The industry was subsequently stunned, but never bored, by his behavior. His standard outfit was usually filthy blue jeans and a T-shirt. His demeanor was consistent: sullen and moody. His eating habits were not of the Cary Grant school. However, his unconventionality made news. Everybody talked about him, and one friend states that Brando was always aware that his kookiness was "good for business—the Brando business."

While movie magazines and gossip columnists began

referring to him in print as "The Slob," Marlon was also described as "a non-conformist in the grand style, part mud-spattered child, part genius—a harlequin who had not yet been housebroken."

He made uncomplimentary remarks about Hollywood's phony glamour and lack of culture. He was uncooperative during interviews. Hedda Hopper babbled on for half an hour during which Brando "gave exactly one-and-a-half grunts." When Hedda huffily asked if he would like the interview continued at another time, he unhesitatingly answered Yes and walked out.

The other leading columnist of the day was Louella Parsons. Brando referred to her as "The Fat One." "Most of the big stars had wanted to tell off Louella for a long time," notes a Hollywood actress. "He did what we were all afraid to do. We respected him for it."

Brando's personal tastes were considered "uncouth." He preferred his motorcycle to a Jaguar, and dated hash-house waitresses, antagonizing many of Hollywood's well-known beauties anxious to "know Brando better."

His pranks made news. On one occasion he drove down Sunset Boulevard in a convertible with a trick arrow on his head, giving the illusion that he had been shot through the skull.

While he outraged Hollywood's denizens with his non-conformist approach to stardom, they could find no fault with his attitude toward his work. In preparation for *The Men*, Marlon decided he needed firsthand information and training for the role. "Look, I've got it all figured out," he told Stanley Kramer. "I want to go to the hospital and live."

He went to live in a ward with thirty-one paraplegics at the Birmingham Hospital. The men there did not readily accept him at first, suspicious that his action was a publicity stunt. In a short while, however, he had earned their respect and won them over.

On one occasion Brando had done something, in jest, to embarrass one of the men, Herbie Wolf, who had become one of his best friends. The next day, Herbie rolled Brando up in his bed despite Brando's threats to drown him in the swimming pool.

34

"Now, you miserable bastard, suffer," chuckled Wolf.

One evening Brando and his hospital friends, all of them in wheelchairs, of course, went to a local pub. A woman, obviously a crackpot, came over and began lecturing them about their noble sacrifice and the miracles that could be achieved through faith. The men were both annoyed and bored by her remarks. Suddenly she noticed the efforts of Brando. He was clutching desperately at the arms of his chair, trying to raise himself. He fell back exhausted. He tried again, managed to rise, took a couple of faltering steps, and broke into a furious, complicated tap dance. The woman fainted dead away. The men agreed Brando had given a good performance.

A national magazine did a photo layout of Brando at the hospital in training for the film. In one shot he was pictured lying on the floor, trying to get up after a fall without using any muscles below the waist. The process involved pulling himself around on his stomach, then, letting his feet drag, using his shoulders and arms to lift himself slowly with the help of parallel bars.

As shooting on the film progressed, Kramer began to wonder whether he had chosen the right actor for the role because Brando was mumbling his lines and not projecting to the other actors. But then came the bedside scene with Teresa Wright. "He summoned the emotion he had been withholding," remembered Kramer. "Everyone was destroyed. Suddenly he had bite and power." Wright was moved to tears.

Asked about his hardest scene in this film, Brando said, "None of it was easy. The hardest was where Teresa first comes to the hospital. I just didn't feel it. But old man Adler, old Jacob, taught me something once I've never forgotten. To hold back twenty per cent and you're always being honest with an audience. They're the actors, you know. Try to show more than you have to give and they catch on right away."

Brando's work habits were commendable. He never was late on the set, didn't indulge in tantrums, and never required endless retakes.

The Men opened at Radio City Music Hall in May 1950. Although the film wasn't big at the box office it was with critics. "Brando plays the crippled Wilozek with much the same sullen tenseness that made his Kowalski a memorable figure," wrote *Newsweek*. *Time* said, "Broadway's Brando does a magnificent job. His halting, mumbled delivery, glowering silences and expert simulation of paraplegics do not suggest acting at all; they look chillingly like the real thing."

But Brando had alienated the Hollywood establishment and they ignored his talent. He didn't receive an Oscar nomination for *The Men*.

Many established actors disliked and disapproved of Brando's "new" approach to his craft. "The Method" was hardly new, of course, but it was new to old-line Hollywood. It was a naturalistic school of acting in which the actor is supposed to cease being himself and become the character. Director Alfred Hitchcock, one of those who doesn't enjoy working with Method actors, was once asked by a highly paid actor what the motivation was for one bit of business during a scene. Hitchcock dryly told him: "The motivation is your salary."

While Brando annoyed Hollywood society and columnists, his potential as a money-maker was what mattered to the hard-shell producers and studio bigwigs. In the words of an ex-production executive: "If you can make money for 'em, they'll let you shit on their living room rug. And thank you for it."

The toughest of the tough, Columbia Pictures potentate Harry Cohn, said a few years later: "There's nothing we can do about these star deals. If Marlon Brando will make a deal with me tomorrow for fifty percent of the picture, I'd kiss him."

Brando wasn't yet getting a percentage of the profits but he commanded a hefty $75,000 from Jack Warner, on another one-picture deal, to re-create Stanley Kowalski in the film version of *Streetcar*. His costar in the role of Blanche would be Scarlett O'Hara herself, Academy Award winner Vivien Leigh. Brando's stage *Streetcar* costars, Karl Malden and Kim Hunter, were signed to re-create their roles for the film. The director: Elia

Kazan. (Kazan had held out for Brando, and according to one source, had initially wanted Olivia de Havilland for Blanche.)

Shooting went smoothly but there was one incident recalled by Karl Malden. Malden's biggest scene in the film was during the poker game and when shooting of the sequence began, Marlon kept "horsing around." He was stepping on most of Malden's lines. "He was the star," Karl said, "and he could get away with it. But I also knew that he was a nice guy and was probably not thinking of what he was doing to my part. I put it to him straight. I said, 'You've got fifty sides and can toss them away and still register. If I lose one of mine, I've got nothing.' He understood right away. 'I never thought of it that way,' he said to me. And when that sequence was shot, I got more than was coming to me."

Streetcar was a charmed production. A smash hit in every way. Brando's torn T-shirt became a nationwide symbol of masculinity, and his brooding, seething silences and bursts of mumbled dialogue established a new acting style for films.

Brando received his first Oscar nomination. With this, only his second film, his name became a household word and the cry "Stell-a" was heard throughout the land. Mimics and comedians added Brando imitations to their repertoires. The film was an international hit and established Marlon Brando as a major motion picture star throughout the world.

Vivien Leigh won the Oscar as Best Actress, Karl Malden and Kim Hunter won as Best Supporting Actor and Actress. Brando lost to Humphrey Bogart in *The African Queen.*

The Brando cult began to mushroom. Youngsters imitated his style of dress (still mainly blue jeans and T-shirt) and speech pattern. One magazine captioned a photo of him in which he wore the famous torn T-shirt: "He beat up Vivien Leigh in 'A Streetcar Named Desire' and led a group of younger actors into imitating his torn shirt, sullen body-builder acting."

For $100,000 Brando signed for *Viva Zapata!*, another role which would add to his image as a rebel. He played Emiliano Zapata, the legendary Mexican folk hero, a man of the people who rose to lead them against the oppressors running the Mexican government. Although Zapata is killed his legend lives on: "They'll never get him," says one character. "You cannot capture the river. You cannot kill the wind." Another character answers: "He is not a river, and he is not the wind. He is a man, but they still can't kill him."

During filming of *Zapata,* Brando became "friendly" with a stunning Mexican woman who had a bit part in the picture. Her name was Maria Louisa Castenada, professional name Movita. She had enjoyed brief celebrity in the middle 1930s as the Tahitian girl in the original film of *Mutiny on the Bounty.* In private life she was the estranged wife of Jack Doyle, a former Irish heavyweight. She soon became Brando's constant companion and number one "date." She sported a flashy engagement ring but there was no announced engagement or wedding plans. Many said they were merely good friends and pointed out, somewhat jealously, that Movita was considerably older than twenty-eight-year-old Marlon. However she was really only six years older than he. His relationship with her was not a momentary fling. Their volatile love affair would last for many stormy years.

Zapata was another hit. Marlon received another Oscar nomination. He and director Kazan were praised by reviewers, and years later Kazan said that many of the bits of business et al. that made Marlon's portrayal of Zapata unique and memorable were Marlon's own inventions.

Many of Hollywood's old and not-so-old guard still couldn't understand how this actor, not handsome-pretty in the way Hollywood was used to thinking of its heroes, and who mumbled his way through his parts and was never seen at the right places with the right people, how, they wondered, could he attract such a large following among the fans?

Despite the barrage of disapproval, Brando would not conform to "accepted" Hollywood ways. He continued to be his own man, asserting his independence and individuality. According to a friend, "Marlon always reacts opposite to what people expect. If they—that Hollywood group—had accepted him im-

Movita at seventeen, circa 1935. She didn't make it in films.

mediately, T-shirt, bad manners and all, he would have reverted to a business suit and tie so fast they wouldn't have known what happened."

A retired motion picture company executive talks freely today about his Brando encounters. "I found him a surly son-of-a-bitch. He did things to goad you. But then again, I find most actors are sons-of-bitches. They impose their ill behavior on you because they know you have to take it.

"Did you ever watch Brando in action at an interview? If he was in a charming mood, you could bet your eyeballs that the journalist would go away thinking that every 'bad' story about Brando was a load of crap. When in actuality that charm act she was witnessing was a performance. It was, in my opinion, the way he felt like coming on at the moment.

"Brando is no different than any other actor off-camera. It's a constant performance and God help the people who have to put up with it."

By this time many of Hollywood's "name" actresses were chasing after Marlon, since he obviously wasn't going to pursue them. One was Shelley Winters, prior to her marriage to Vittorio Gassman. Although Brando and Shelley "dated," the romance didn't last. "Marlon could be a very physical person," remembers an acquaintance. "When he reacted to a spectacular broad it was only for a lay or two. He preferred relationships where he could be gentle, loving. Trouble was many of the girls he bedded down wanted him to be Stanley Kowalski. On the occasions when he wasn't, boy were they disappointed."

Brando received a high bedroom rating from bosomy blonde personality-turned-writer Liz Renay, who recalled him fondly in her autobiography, *My Face for the World to See*.

Because of the certain sameness of character possessed by Marlon's movie roles up to this point, many were convinced that he was a one-type actor, a Johnny-One-Note. All he could play, they maintained, was the part of a mumbling, rough, brutal, antisocial hero. Brando, true to form, delivered an unexpected coup.

Shelley Winters: A Brando date and
friend but never a "serious" romance

He signed with MGM to star in *Julius Caesar*, under Joseph Mankiewicz's direction. There was much speculation as to whether Brando would play the role as an offshoot of Messrs. Wilozek-Kowalski. Jokes circulated on how he would deliver the "Friends, Romans, countrymen" speech. Marlon, however, surprised all. His interpretation of Antony was articulate, restrained yet intense. He performed Shakespeare with consummate technique and received his third consecutive Oscar nomination. This time he lost to William Holden in *Stalag 17*.

Caesar director Mankiewicz strongly contradicts reports that Marlon was "difficult to work with." Mankiewicz found exactly the opposite to be true, and states that both he and Brando were far too busy on the film for either to have had time to be "difficult."

Hot Blood, retitled *The Wild One*, brought Brando back with Stanley Kramer for a role that would forever, for better or worse, ensure his rebel image. Brando portrayed the tough, black-leather-jacketed leader of a motorcycle gang in this, one of the most controversial films ever made. It was based on a short story, "The Cyclist's Raid," which in turn was based on an actual event in the late 1940s when thousands of members of a motorcycle club held a riotous convention in a small California town. The theme and mood of the picture made it one of the most talked-about films of the early fifties. *The Wild One* set the tone for the next twenty years of films about youth gangs and motorcyclists.

"What are you rebelling against?" a character in the film asks Brando. "What have you got?" is his reply.

While the picture tried to explore the underlying problems that produced these social misfits, it failed as a drama of social significance since most people interpreted it as a film about violence.

Brando hated the final picture: "We started out to explain the hipster psychology, but somewhere along the way we went off the track. The result was that instead of finding out why young people tend to bunch into groups that seek expression in violence, all we did was show the violence."

In England, *The Wild One* was considered dangerous since "it might incite youth to riot." What bothered many critics was that the violence in the film seemed to them a form of sexuality. Indeed, this was one of the first Hollywood-produced movies in which the characters were overtly sexual.

Whereas Brando had made the torn T-shirt a sex symbol in 1951, with *The Wild One* in 1954 his black leather jacket and motorcycle became symbols of virility. (Even though Brando was a motorcycle enthusiast offscreen, he was not allowed to do most of his own riding in the picture.)

Brando returned to the east to appear in a summer stock production of Shaw's *Arms and the Man* at the Theatre-by-the-Sea in Matunuck, Rhode Island. A friend recalls, "Marlon was sick of the West Coast movie schmucks and wanted to prove to himself that he could still act." While in the play he met and became romantically involved with actress Janice Mars.

Arms was only a two-week run and Marlon accepted nonstar salary so the limited budget could afford him. Afterward he sailed for Europe and his first love, Paris.

★ 4 ★

It is ironic and typical of show business that two of Brando's most important roles were originally designated for other actors. Garfield had turned down *Streetcar* and Frank Sinatra was set to play Terry Malloy in *On the Waterfront*.

Elia Kazan has said that from the beginning he wanted Brando for *Waterfront*. But Brando was unavailable at the time they needed a definite commitment, and producer Sam Spiegel promised the role to Sinatra, who was hot on the comeback trail after *From Here to Eternity*. Sinatra surely seemed right for the role of the knocked-around ex-boxer. Besides, Frank was from Hoboken, and the Hoboken, New Jersey, docks were the background for *On the Waterfront*.

The idea for the film, which was about union corruption among New York dock workers, dated back to the late 1940s when Elia Kazan and Arthur Miller talked about collaborating on a story. However, Kazan subsequently testified before the House Un-American Activities Committee, which in the late forties and early fifties investigated Communist infiltration in the motion picture industry. Because of his testimony, his friendship with Miller, who had refused to testify, cooled. Their idea for a film was abandoned but not forgotten.

In 1950 screenwriter Budd Schulberg began writing a screenplay based on reporter Malcolm Johnson's Pulitzer Prize-winning series of articles about murder and racketeering in the New York waterfront union. Three years later, Schulberg and

Kazan got together on the project and approached Sam Spiegel to produce the film.

There is a theory that *On the Waterfront* is Schulberg's and Kazan's defense of their positions on informing (Schulberg too had testified before the House Un-American Activities Committee). It is interesting to note that years later Miller's play and subsequent movie *A View From the Bridge* also had an underlying theme on informing. While in *On the Waterfront* informing is "good," in *View from the Bridge* it is "bad."

When *On the Waterfront* went to Brando, Sinatra was furious with Sam Spiegel. He felt he "had been screwed" and never spoke to him again.

Marlon was miserable while making the film. His private life was coming apart. His affair with Movita ended abruptly

Movita in the early 1950s.
She would become Marlon's second wife.

when she walked out on him. In the words of a friend: "She decided she had had enough."

Spiegel contends that Marlon gives his best performances when he's personally unhappy. That certainly proved correct in the case of *On the Waterfront*. Almost everyone considers it his best performance.

One of the most memorable scenes in the film occurs when Brando confronts his brother (played by Rod Steiger), a crooked lawyer for the racketeers. "Oh, Charley, Charley," he tells him, "you didn't understand. I coulda had class. I coulda been a contender. I coulda been somebody instead of a bum— which is what I am."

Brando's memories of that particular scene and of the film itself are unsentimental:

"That was a seven-take scene, and I didn't like the way it was written. Lot of dissension going on there. I was fed up with the whole picture. All the location stuff was in New Jersey, and it was the dead of winter—the cold, Christ! And I was having problems at the time. Women trouble. That scene. Let me see. There were seven takes because Rod Steiger couldn't stop crying. He's one of those actors who loves to cry. We kept doing it over and over. But I can't remember just when, just how it crystallized itself for me. The first time I saw 'Waterfront,' in a projection room with Gadge [Kazan], I thought it was so terrible I walked out without even speaking to him."

As soon as *Waterfront* was finished, Brando had to report to Hollywood to begin work on *The Egyptian* for Fox. It was a CinemaScope-Technicolor spectacle, large on production values but, in the opinion of some, small in the script department. After several days on the set, Brando walked out and returned to New York to see his psychiatrist. The next day, Dr. Mittelmann telegraphed the studio to tell them that Brando would be unable to return to work for ten weeks.

Soon after this occurred, a man appeared at Brando's apartment on West Fifty-seventh Street, posing as an official from the Motion Picture Academy, saying that he had to speak to him about his nomination. Brando, thinking, of course, that it had to do with his Oscar nomination for *Julius Caesar,* opened the door. The man was a process server who slapped a summons into Brando's hand. Then, on February 16, 1954, Twentieth Century Fox Corporation filed, in Federal court in New York City, a damage claim for $2,000,000 against Marlon Brando. The complaint alleged that Brando "refuses to perform under his current contract and contemplates working for others." It further characterized Brando as an actor with unique and extraordinary skill and ability, implying Brando would be impossible to replace. Fox maintained that Brando had signed two contracts with them, agreeing, under the terms of one contract, to star in *The Egyptian.* They said that it was costing them $10,000 a day and that accrued losses to date amounted to $1,500,000. Brando had no comment.

Meanwhile, Marlon had received word that his mother was ailing. Soon the news became grim, as she took a turn for the worse. Brando rushed to her bedside and was there when she died on March 31, 1954.

A short time later Brando returned to Fox, this time to star as Napoleon in *Desirée.* It is widely believed that he accepted this role in return for Fox's withdrawing the suit against him (Edmond Purdom had played *The Egyptian*). Some claim that Marlon returned to Fox because he had made a promise to his dying mother that he would try to get along with people.

Industryites began to detect, or so they thought, signs of change in Marlon. A couple of Hollywood columnists even claimed credit for the change. One actor who had worked with him said it was not change but development, adding: "Nobody, nothing, no amount of money can *make* him behave. He's got to be his own master, even though he may not yet have mastered himself. A paradox. Brando's riddled with paradoxes. *And* conflicts. *And* inner problems. An extraordinarily complicated Joe trying to understand himself, to uncover his own destiny. Not six but a thousand characters in search of their author."

When *Desirée* was completed, Brando canceled a trip to Europe in order to spend some time with his father. He made every attempt now that his mother was gone to get along with Marlon Sr. Concerning his father's indifference to him as a child, Marlon said: "I've accepted that now. We're friends. Now —we get along."

Brando Sr. was an astute businessman. He had been investing Marlon's money since the *Streetcar* days, and over the years the sums got larger and larger. Brando Jr. continued to send the greater part of his salary to his father for the Marsdo (Marlon's dough) Holding Company. This money went into a few oil wells and large numbers of cattle in Nebraska. It was pointed out that if Brando retired at this point, he could live comfortably for the rest of his life.

The Brandos were planning to become partners in a production company, named for Marlon's mother: Pennebaker Productions. At last it seemed that father and son had something in common.

Later in the fall, Marlon finally took his trip to Europe. In November 1954, an engagement announcement appeared in a local newspaper of the French town of Toulon stating: "Madame and Monsieur Paul Berenger of Bandol are happy to announce the engagement of their daughter Josanne to Monsieur Marlon Brando." By the next day, every available American reporter in Europe had converged on the small town. For the next several days, Marlon and Josanne were followed everywhere they went. Reporters doubted his sincerity until he purchased the engagement ring. Fans in America doubted it too, even after he had bought the ring, assuming the romance to be one of Brando's passing fancies.

Who was Josanne Mariana Berenger? Earlier, in New York, Brando had met Josanne, aged nineteen, stepdaughter of a French fisherman, at a party at Stella Adler's. One of the party-goers recalls that Josanne, "like all the girls there, was trying to catch his eye. He ignored her, was even rude. She thought she didn't stand a chance but as she was about to leave he blocked her exit and said, 'You're coming with me.'"

According to one of Marlon's ex-girl-friends, "Marlon

Brandos Sr. and Jr. in the mid-1950s

Marlon and Josanne Berenger, the French girl he almost married in the mid-1950s sometimes enjoys humiliating women. I heard that on the second night he dated Josanne he told her he was bringing someone to dinner. It turned out to be another girl everyone knew he was balling."

Josanne, previously a model in France, had worked as a governess for a New York family. She began to date Brando. Few people knew she was in Hollywood while he was filming *Desirée*. She was on the set almost every day, sitting inconspicuously off to one side. Hardly anyone noticed her. Then, just as quietly, she returned to France. No one knew or suspected anything serious was going on between them. Hence, the absolute surprise at news of the engagement.

When Brando returned to America in December aboard the liner *United States* he told reporters, "It is not a publicity stunt, and I do intend to marry the girl . . . in the summer." Asked the difference between foreign and American girls, he bristled, "In choosing a wife, I don't think it's important to question her nationality, providing she's not Joe Stalin's cousin."

Later, at his hotel, after a meeting with Josanne, he announced that there had been a change in their plans. The wedding, he said, would take place sometime that month.

But take place it did not, and Brando returned to the West Coast to begin work on *Guys and Dolls*. Josanne was, at different times, with him, then reported to be back in New York, in Brando's vacant apartment, then back with him in Hollywood. On the basis of her relationship with Brando, she appeared on television, was interviewed by numerous magazines and newspapers, and began studying dramatics with a view toward an acting career. She eventually had bit parts on Broadway and in summer stock. In Hollywood she had a few bit parts, mostly roles calling for a foreign accent. But she had lost her big prize.

Brando switched from unknowns to celebrities. His name was linked, at various times, with Rita Moreno, Susan Cabot, Joan Collins, Francesca Scaffa, Katy Jurado, and Pier Angeli.

Pier Angeli,
lovely Italian actress,
was another Brando date.
She eventually married
singer Vic Damone.

Marlon and actress Joan Collins were romantically involved for a brief spell.

The year 1955 was golden for Brando. He was at the very top. *Waterfront* was a box-office giant and the reviews, both of Brando and the film, were brilliant. The prizes started rolling in. Brando won the Golden Globe from the Hollywood Foreign Correspondents. He was awarded the New York Newspaper Guild's Annual Page One Award. And then, on the evening of March 30, 1955, he was awarded Hollywood's highest honor— the Oscar. It had been his fourth consecutive nomination. The coveted statuette was presented to him by Hollywood's venerable female rebel, Bette Davis, who later said: "I was thrilled that Marlon Brando was the winner. He and I had a lot in common. He too had made many enemies. He too is a perfectionist."

Eva Marie Saint, a little-known stage actress, had made her film debut in *On the Waterfront*. She won the Oscar as Best Supporting Actress, Kazan won Best Director and the film won Oscars for writer Budd Schulberg and cinematographer Boris Kaufman. Even though it was a time when Hollywood was promoting CinemaScope, Cinerama, 3-D, and Technicolor, Kazan, Spiegel, Schulberg, and Brando had collaborated to bring forth a black and white film that combined commercial success, social significance, and artistic values.

Brando surprised Hollywood by appearing at the Academy Awards ceremony resplendently yet conservatively arrayed in a dark dress suit. He smiled at reporters. Hedda Hopper claimed, "He almost kissed me."

Brando was the subject of an Edward R. Murrow "Person to Person" interview on nationwide TV. Later, in May 1955, he was chosen as the leading actor of 1954 by British filmgoers. He was given the annual award of *Picturegoer* magazine.

Though Brando's attire had become more conventional (some attributed this to Josanne's influence), his behavior still smacked of the unpredictable. Driving to a picnic with a journalist, Brando sat silently brooding. Suddenly he yelled, "Stop!" The driver slammed on the brakes. Brando leaped out of the car, stared at the sky, and pointed. "Hawks," he whispered. "See how they circle? Aren't they lovely and free? Their movement is so slow and uninterrupted." Then he stared at the hills. "They need rain to make them even richer." The writer recalled that later at the picnic "Brando played with insects, allowing them to crawl over his hands and fingers, studying their coloring and then gently blowing them away."

Marlon's relations with the press remained tenuous. His father once explained, "The reason his press relations will never

Brando, in costume and makeup for his role as Napoleon in *Desirée*, poses with his *On the Waterfront* Oscar and actress Katy Jurado, with whom he was romantically linked.

be any good is that he wants to talk about his work and they want to talk about his private life."

When Marlon *had* to make public appearances, photographers were unavoidable. But he was usually more clever than they. For example, on one occasion he had to appear in Los Angeles Court to answer two warrants for traffic violations. The judge cleared the courtroom and Brando told the photographers waiting outside, "My chances of ducking you guys on the way out are fifty-fifty. There are two doors out of this joint. Try and catch me."

Brando pleaded guilty to the violations and was fined forty dollars. Then he skillfully avoided America's paparazzi by dodging through the judge's chambers, cutting through two more courtrooms and leaping out of the building through a window. The one photographer who heeded Brando's warning waited outside the building instead of in the hallway and got a shot of Marlon frantically dashing toward the parking lot.

While Brando's films had all been hits, Pennebaker Productions was having some minor troubles. Its first scheduled production, *To Tame a Land,* did not start because of script difficulties. Paramount Pictures, however, having faith in the company, extended their association with Pennebaker to include a second film about United Nations research workers kidnapped by warrior natives in Southeast Asia.

Brando planned to travel with associate producer George Englund and writer Stewart Stern to make a firsthand survey of Southeast Asia. "I am going along to select and perhaps investigate any situation that will bring forth story material," declared Brando. To the amusement of some industryites he added, "I'll also serve as a kind of diplomat for the movie industry. By circumstance rather than intention."

Brando limited himself to one picture a year from this point on. Hollywood was still talking about him, but in a different way. Not only was "The Slob" gone, since Brando now appeared more often in conventional dress, but he also began to be seen in Hollywood "society." When photographed by newsmen he was smiling and laughing instead of sulking and brooding.

Much to Marlon's displeasure, sulking and brooding on screen had been taken over by a new, younger screen idol, Elia Kazan's discovery James Dean.

Whatever publicity stunts Brando had been accused of in the early 1950s, Dean now outdid him. Acutely publicity conscious, he dressed more sloppily than Brando, was even more

Brando with Brando admirer, James Dean

tactless, and, with his all-night carousing, motorcycle riding, and race-car driving, was considered even wilder than Brando. He became known as "the complete nonconformist" in Hollywood.

"The major difference between Brando's behavior and Dean's was that Brando's was very often a put-on," notes a director who knew them both. "If people didn't realize that, Marlon always did. But Dean was self-destructive. Masochistic. It was no act with him—he was sick."

Discussing Dean's widely acclaimed first film, *East of Eden,* Brando noted: "Jim and I worked together at Actors Studio in New York, and I have great respect for his talent. However, in that film, Mr. Dean appears to be wearing my last year's wardrobe and using my last year's talent."

It was reported that Dean and Brando used the same psychoanalyst and thus further cemented the theory that Dean was a carbon copy of Brando. Dean's retort was, "I have my own personal rebellion and don't have to rely on Brando's."

One critic raised an interesting point: "Those who have seen 'East of Eden' say that if you close your eyes while Dean is speaking, you'll swear you are listening to Brando. Since 'Eden' was directed by Elia Kazan, some people are wondering just how much of Brando is really Kazan."

The controversy ended abruptly when twenty-four-year-old Dean was killed in an automobile accident.

Warner Brothers put together a documentary on Dean's life and wanted Brando to narrate it. To industry astonishment, he actually gave the matter serious consideration. "I think I might. Maybe not, though," Marlon reflected at the time. Giving insight to his character he continued: "I get excited about something, but it never lasts more than seven minutes. Seven minutes exactly. That's my limit. I never know why I get up in the morning. . . . But I'm really considering this Dean thing. It could be important."

Had he been close to Dean? "No, Dean was never a friend of mine. That's not why I may do the narration job. I hardly knew him. But he had an *idée fixe* about me. Whatever I did he did. He was always trying to get close to me. He used to call up . . . I'd listen to him talking to the answering service, asking for me, leaving messages. But I never spoke up. I never called him back. No, when I finally met Dean, it was at a party. Where he was throwing himself around, acting the madman. So I spoke to him. I took him aside and asked him didn't he know he was sick? That he needed help. . . . He listened to me. He knew he was sick. I gave him the name of an analyst, and he went. And at least his *work* improved. Toward the end, I think he was beginning to find his own way as an actor. But this glorifying of Dean is all wrong. That's why I believe the documentary could be important. To show he wasn't a hero; show what he really was—just a lost boy trying to find himself. That ought to be done, and I'd like to do it—maybe as a kind of expiation for some of my own sins. Like making 'The Wild One.'. . . But who knows? Seven minutes is my limit."

Brando didn't do the narration. Martin Gabel got the job and the documentary, released in October 1957, did indeed glorify Dean and add to the Dean legend.

Guys and Dolls, costarring Frank Sinatra, was a hit at the box office despite mediocre reviews and the dullness of the film. The role was another departure for Brando. "The only reason I did it was to work in a lighter color—yellow. Before that, the brightest color I'd played was red. From red down. Brown. Gray. Black." Comparing Brando and Sinatra on the set, an industry observer said, "Sinatra plays God to his entourage. Brando doesn't."

According to one source, who subsequently became one of Marlon's detractors, Brando disliked Sinatra because "he felt threatened by him. Frank was a great talent and individual but Marlon usually referred to him as 'a singer.'"

Joseph Mankiewicz directed the film. When Mankiewicz had heard, early in negotiations, that Brando was reluctant to do musical comedy, he wired Marlon that there was no need to be apprehensive. Mankiewicz pointed out that he, too, had never done a musical.

There is an amusing story concerning the engagement of *Guys and Dolls* in Germany, where Brando had always been a favorite. For this film his speaking voice was, as usual, dubbed in German by a gravel-voiced baritone. However, the musical numbers, in which Brando did his own singing, were left intact. When German audiences heard, for the first time, Marlon's rather high-pitched voice, they realized the voice they had fallen in love with as part of the Brando mystique actually belonged to an unseen actor. Marlon's popularity in Germany momentarily took quite a nose dive.

Marlon was intent on avoiding typecasting. For his next picture he decided on a comedy, *Teahouse of the August Moon,* shot partly on location in Japan. The role of the wily oriental Sakini was in effect a character role for Brando, and would be the actor's only attempt at such a departure until *The Godfather* sixteen years later.

Next came *Sayonara.* That would be an experience none of those connected with the film will ever forget.

Sayonara was largely filmed on location in Japan. Brando liked the country and the people. He observed at the time, "They kill me. They really kill me. The kids, too. Don't you think they're wonderful, don't you love them—Japanese kids?"

Brando was ensconced at the Western-style Miyako Hotel. His domain there consisted of two rooms, a bath, and glassed-in sun porch. His belongings usually cluttered the premises: clothing, cameras, typewriter, tape recorder, and an electric heater functioning at top capacity. Food, some partly eaten, was here and there. Also scattered about were books—*The Outsider* by Colin Wilson, books on Buddhist prayer, Zen meditation, Yoga, Hindu mysticism. Everything but fiction. Brando claimed he never read fiction and had never opened a novel.

He was at this time writing an original film script—*A Burst of Vermilion.* A young man identified as "a fellow that's helping Marlon with his writing" was one of what the film company referred to as "Brando's gang." The group consisted of

The press turns out for a rare event: a Marlon Brando press conference. (This one in Tokyo at the time of *Teahouse of the August Moon.*)

Marlon Brando Sr., a pretty brunette secretary, Miss Levin, and a private makeup man.

Not many stars of the day could insist that economy-conscious film companies pay the expenses of their entourages. "Ordinarily we wouldn't put up with it," said a Warner Brothers spokesman referring to "Brando's gang." "All the demands he makes. Except—well, this picture just *had* to have a big star. Your star—that's the only thing that counts at the box office."

Marlon's entourage served a practical purpose. It was an effective social buffer against the rest of the *Sayonara* company, most of whom resented it, since they "wanted to get to know the guy." However, Brando preferred to be by himself. Between scenes he would read philosophy or write in his notebook. At the end of the day he wouldn't socialize but returned to his hotel. His attitude was described as "friendly remoteness."

After two weeks of filming, director Joshua Logan, noted as one of filmdom's most talented diplomats ("Marlon's the most exciting person I've met since Garbo. A genius . . ."), was forced to admit: "But I don't know what he's like. I don't know anything about him."

It was only the beginning.

By now Marlon was having problems with his weight. He had to trim off ten pounds before starting *Sayonara* but soon into the film he had put back more than twenty. "I've *got* to lose weight," he noted. (While compulsive eating and weight control would prove problematic, friends noted that because of his background there was one problem Marlon would never be plagued by: alcohol.)

He was more intensely self-absorbed than ever and, like all such people, he tended not to listen when others were talking. But, "People around me never say anything," he complained. "They just seem to want to hear what I have to say. That's why I do all the talking." He was still unhappy. "The last eight, nine years of my life have been a mess. Maybe the last two have been a little better. Less rolling in the trough of the wave. . . . But still, the last eight, nine years I've been pretty mixed up, a mess pretty much. . . ."

Although unhappy, Brando was by this point very sure of himself. He looked at people with *such* assurance, with what has been described as "a pitying expression" for them on his face, that it inspired opposite reactions from friends: "Marlon is really a very *spiritual* person, wise and very sincere; you can see it in his eyes," said a young actress. "The way he looks at you," said another friend, "like he was so damn sorry for you—doesn't it make you want to cut your throat?"

Was Brando *always* unhappy? "I remember one April I

was in Sicily. A hot day, and flowers everywhere. I like flowers, the ones that smell. Gardenias. Anyway, it was April and I was in Sicily, and I went off by myself. Lay down in this field of flowers. Went to sleep. That made me happy. I was happy *then*. . . ."

Would he return to the stage at this point? "Why should I? The movies have a greater potential. They can be a factor for good. For moral development. At least some can—the kind of movies I want to do. . . . What's so hot about New York? What's so hot about working for [theatrical producers] Cheryl Crawford and Robert Whitehead? Anyway, what would I be in? There aren't any parts for me."

Although he was interested only in making significant movies, "Of course, movies *date* so quickly. I saw 'Streetcar' the other day and it was already an old-fashioned picture. Still, movies do have the greatest potential. You can say important things to a lot of people. About discrimination and hate and prejudice. I want to make pictures that explore the themes current in the world today. In terms of entertainment. That's why I started my own production company."

A Burst of Vermilion was planned as the first venture for Pennebaker Productions. "It's a western," said Marlon. "Christ, the only thing is will I ever be able to look my friends in the face again? Seriously, though, the first picture *has* to make money. Otherwise, there won't be another. I'm nearly broke. No, no kidding. [He was being paid $300,000 plus a percentage for *Sayonara*.] I spent a year and two hundred thousand dollars of my own money trying to get some writer to come up with a decent script. Which used my ideas. The last one, it was so terrible I said I can do better myself. I'm going to direct it, too."

As for producing, "What does a producer do except cast? I know as much about casting as anyone does, and that's all producing is. Casting." Many in the industry would rightfully disagree with this statement.

"But seriously, 'Burst' *isn't* just cowboys-and-Indians stuff. It's about this Mexican boy—hatred and discrimination. What happens to a community when those things exist."

63

Brando had told the press he had contracted to do *Sayonara* because "it strikes very precisely at prejudices that serve to limit our progress toward a peaceful world. Underneath the romance, it attacks prejudices that exist on the part of the Japanese as well as on our part." He also was making the film since it would allow him the "invaluable opportunity" of working with Joshua Logan who would teach him "what to do and what not to do."

Brando had a change of heart after the film had started. "Oh, 'Sayonara,' I love it! This wondrous hearts-and-flowers nonsense that was supposed to be a serious picture about Japan. So what difference does it make? I'm just doing it for the money anyway, money to put in the kick for my own company . . .

"Back in California, I sat through twenty-two hours of script conferences. Logan said to me, 'We welcome any suggestions you have, Marlon. Any changes you want to make, you just make them. If there's anything you don't like—why, rewrite it, Marlon, write it your own way. . . .

"*Rewrite?* Man, I rewrote the whole damn script. And now out of that they're going to use maybe eight lines. I give up. I'm going to walk through the part, and that's that. Sometimes I think nobody knows the difference anyway. For the first few days on the set, I tried to act. But then I made an experiment. In this scene, I tried to do everything wrong I could think of. Grimaced and rolled my eyes, put in all kinds of gestures and expressions that had no relation to the part I'm supposed to be playing. What did Logan say? He just said, 'It's wonderful! Print it.'"

A great story, but one must keep in mind that Brando constantly told his friends, "I only mean forty percent of what I say."

If Brando felt so contemptuous of *Sayonara* and Joshua Logan, Logan, an exceedingly enthusiastic man who had spent two years preparing the production, didn't acknowledge it because he was thrilled about how the film was going and went so far as to say, "Marlon says he's never been as happy with a company as he is with us." On another occasion he said, "I've never worked with such an exciting, inventive actor. So pliable. He takes direction beautifully and yet he always has something to add. He's made up this Southern accent for the part; I never would have thought of it myself, but, well, it's exactly right—it's perfection."

Logan was hardly insensitive or stupid. He began to realize that his relationship with Brando lacked something. But he felt the reason was that they hadn't really worked on the big scenes yet to be filmed back in California. That's when things would crystallize between the director and his star. "The interior stuff, the dramatic scenes," said Logan. "Brando's going to be great—we'll get along fine." Meanwhile Logan had other production problems to occupy his mind at this point.

Among other things, Logan was particularly concerned about two other principals in the cast: Miiko Taka, an unknown with no dramatic training who got the role Logan had wanted Audrey Hepburn for; and Red Buttons, the comedian who was embarking on a career as a dramatic actor. Regarding their performances Logan felt "We'll get away with it. As much as possible, I'll just keep their faces straight and their mouths shut. Anyway, Brando, he's going to be so great *he'll* give us what we need."

Brando, however, had other ideas: "I give up. I'm going to give up. I'm going to sit back. Enjoy Japan."

Marlon's penchant for pranks nearly gave Logan a heart seizure. With only three days left to shoot, Marlon came to the set with his arm in a sling. "Don't blame my stand-in," he said, "we were just wrestling around. It's my fault. I started it."

"Is it broken?" asked Logan.

"I think so."

Production was over schedule. "Can't you remove the sling for a few minutes at a time?" begged Logan.

"No. The doctor says I must keep my arm in the sling at all times or I'll be crippled for life."

Logan was beside himself. "If I change the camera set-up, so the sling doesn't show, could you move your fingers a little bit?"

"Well, I reckon I could." He then began twitching his fingers violently and roared with laughter.

Logan later admitted that to keep Marlon contented, "We put him with twenty young Japanese girls and at times he was happy."

Brando was fascinated by mystical subjects. The idea of a person leading a spiritual, unworldly existence totally intrigued him. He was dumbfounded and upset when, one day during *Sayonara,* "we were working in a temple and one of the monks came over and asked me for an autographed picture. Now, *what* would a monk want with my autograph? A picture of me?"

At a Tokyo press conference he said he was pleased to be back in Japan because it would give him another opportunity to "investigate the influence of Buddhism on Japanese thought, the determining cultural factor."

"What I'd like to do," he said on a later occasion, "I'd like to talk to someone who *knows* about these things. Because I've seriously considered—I've very *seriously* thought about—throwing the whole thing up. This business of being a successful actor. What's the point, if it doesn't evolve into anything? All right, you're a success. At last you're *accepted,* you're welcome everywhere. But that's it, that's all there is to it, it just doesn't lead anywhere. You're just sitting on a pile of candy gathering thick layers of—*crust.* Too much success can ruin you as surely as too much failure. Of course, you can't *always* be a failure. Not and survive. Van Gogh! There's an example of what can happen when a person never receives any recognition. You stop relating; it puts you outside. But I guess success does that too."

How would Marlon follow his quest for a life that "led somewhere"?

"Well, when I get back to Hollywood, what I *will* do, I'll fire my secretary and move back into a smaller house. I won't have a cook or maid. Just a cleaning woman who comes in twice a week. But wherever the house is, it has to have a *fence.* On account of the people with pencils. You don't know what it's like. The people with pencils. I need a fence to keep them out. I suppose there's nothing I can do about the telephone. It's tapped. Mine is. When I talk to my friends, we speak French. Or else a kind of bop lingo we make up."

At his hotel Brando's quarters were directly below those of Red Buttons and his wife. "Sh-h-h!" whispered Marlon to a visitor one evening as Buttons and his wife arrived home. "Keep your voice down. *They* can hear everything. This place is made of paper."

Brando admired and respected few Hollywood actors. "Spencer Tracy is the kind of actor I like to watch. The way he holds back, *holds* back—then darts in to make his point, darts back. Tracy, Muni, Cary Grant. They know what they're doing. You can learn from them.

"Acting is such a tenuous thing. A fragile, shy thing that a sensitive director can help lure out of you. Now, in movie acting the important, the *sensitive* moment comes around the third take of a scene; by then you just need a whisper from the director to crystallize it for you. Gadge [nickname for Elia Kazan] can usually do it. He's wonderful with actors."

During the period when Marlon was making *Sayonara,* a friend observed: "Marlon always turns against whatever he's working on. Some element of it. Either the script or the director or somebody in the cast. Not always because of anything very rational—just because it seems to comfort him to be dissatisfied, let off steam about something. It's part of his pattern. Take 'Sayonara.' A dollar gets you ten he'll develop a hoss on it somewhere along the line. A hoss on Logan, maybe. Maybe against Japan—the whole damn country. He loves Japan *now*. But with Marlon you never know from one minute to the next."

How did Brando react to this statement? "I ought to keep my mouth shut. Around here, around *Sayonara,* I've let a few people know the way I feel. But I don't always feel the same way two days running."

Regarding his personal life he had reached the point where, "Well, I'd like to be married. I want to have children. . . .

You've got to have love. There's no other reason for living. Men are no different from mice. They're born to perform the same function. Procreate."

Brando loved children. They were always welcome around the set of *Sayonara*. An observer noted that "the slight look of dispensing charitable compassion with which he looked at adults, was absent from his eyes when Marlon spoke and played with children."

"What other reason is there for living?" wondered Brando aloud to a friend. "Except love? That has been my main trouble. My inability to love anyone. . . . I can't. Love anyone. I can't trust anyone enough to give myself to them. But I'm ready. I want it. And I may, I'm almost on the point, I've really got to . . . Because, well, what else is there? That's all it's all about. To love somebody. . . .

"Anyway, I have *friends*. No. No, I don't . . . Oh, sure I do. I have a great many friends. Some I don't hold out on. I let them know what's happening. You have to trust somebody. Well, not all the way. There's nobody I rely on to tell *me* what to do." Did that include his agent, Jay Kanter, of MCA? "Oh, Jay. Jay does what I tell *him* to do."

Exactly how did one become a Brando friend? "I go about it very gently. I circle around and around. I circle. Then, gradually, I come nearer. Then I reach out and touch them—ah, so gently . . . Then, I draw back. Wait a while. Make them wonder. At just the right moment, I move in again. Touch them. Circle. They don't know what's happening. Before they realize it, they're all entangled, involved. I have them. And suddenly, sometimes, I'm all *they* have. A lot of them, you see, are people who don't fit in anywhere; they're not accepted, they've been hurt, crippled one way or another. But I want to help them, and they can focus on me; I'm the duke. Sort of the duke of my domain."

Marlon has always been the epitome of sensitivity. "I can walk into a room where there are a hundred people—if there is *one* person in that room who doesn't like me, I know it and have to get out."

Brando's affinity for children has always been evident. Here he reads nursery rhymes at a children's hospital.

To his friends Brando is "intellectual father and emotional big brother." In the words of his best friend, Wally Cox, Marlon is "a creative philosopher, a very deep thinker . . . a real liberating force for his friends."

However, in Marlon's words: ". . . listen! Don't pay too much attention to what I say. I don't always feel the same way."

Sayonara proved a big hit, critically and commercially. Brando was nominated for an Academy Award. It would be his last Oscar nomination until *The Godfather.*

★ 5 ★

Brando meant what he said about wanting a wife and children. Everyone was caught completely off guard when he married Indian actress Anna Kashfi on October 11, 1957. Brando was thirty-three and nobody expected him to take the plunge, even though rumors of marriage had flown everytime he had more than a few dates with the same person. Furthermore, no announcement had ever been made of the dissolution of his engagement to Josanne.

The wedding was planned with great secrecy so the press wouldn't get wind of it. Actor Sam Gilman, Brando's friend, was set to purchase the wedding ring. But on a last minute whim Brando himself went into downtown Pasadena to buy it. "Leave it to Marlon," muses a friend. "Although it was this top secret event, he went to buy the ring in a flowing Indian robe. Naturally, he was recognized and mobbed."

The wedding took place at the home of Brando's aunt, Mrs. Bette Lindemeyer, in Eagle Rock, California. The ceremony, attended only by members of Brando's immediate family, was performed by the Rev. J. Walker Fiscus, pastor of the nondenominational Little Brown Church of the San Fernando Valley.

The next day brought Brando a brutal surprise. The newlyweds became the center of a Hollywood brouhaha when a factory worker in Wales, William Patrick O'Callaghan, claimed that Anna Kashfi was not Indian. She was, he said, his daughter Joan. (On her license application Miss Kashfi had listed her

Marlon with Anna Kashfi, his first wife. Her Indian looks belied her Irish heritage.

parents as being Devi Kashfi and Selma Ghose of India. Friends
said that her father had died only a few weeks earlier.) Mr. O'Cal-
laghan said that his daughter, a former model, had gone to Holly-
wood a little over a year before to appear with Spencer Tracy in the
movie *The Mountain*. He said Joan had been born in Darjeeling,
India, when he was working there as a supervisor for the Indian
State Railways. Mrs. O'Callaghan firmly stated: "There is no
Indian blood in my family or in my husband's family." Edward
Dmytryk, director of *The Mountain*, revealed that he had known
Miss Kashfi's real name was Irish. But, "I assumed she was Anglo-
Indian." Brando and Miss Kashfi remained unavailable for com-

ment. Behind the scenes there were, to put it mildly, many comments.

Anna, née Joan, obviously understood Brando's penchant for exotic women. "She was deeply in love with him, and did what she felt she had to do to get him to marry her," recalls a Kashfi chum from that period. "She knew that more than anything else he wanted children." Anna was two months pregnant when Brando married her.

After the revelation of Anna's origins, Brando wouldn't speak to the press and, when pressed for a comment, told reporters what they could do to themselves. However, according to an informed source, in private he urged Anna to reveal her origins to his press agents.

"Go on. Tell them."

"You son of a bitch," she snapped. "When they ask you you tell them it's none of their business. But you want me to tell them so they can tell the press." Then she told Marlon what *he* could do to *him*self.

An ironic footnote to the situation was that Brando originally wanted to marry Anna in Arizona but at that time the state forbade mixed marriages.

Brando and Kashfi kept their battles out of the papers until after the birth of their son, Christian Devi, at Cedars of Lebanon Hospital on May 11, 1958.

By now Brando was making *The Young Lions,* directed by Edward Dmytryk. Brando had "higher hopes for this than I have had for any picture I have ever done"

Costarring in the film was Montgomery Clift. Brando and Clift were at odds during production over interpretation of roles. Brando played a Nazi officer and succeeded in making him a sensitive, sympathetic character. He had bleached his hair blond for the role, and some said he resorted to Kowalski for characterization. Clift portrayed a Jewish-American GI who was a martyr in the story. Clift was annoyed with Brando, who was trying to turn his Nazi character into a martyr too. When filming the end of the picture, when the Brando character is shot and

73

staggers down a hill, Brando wanted to fall across a heap of barbed wire, arms outstretched. Clift threatened to walk off the set, and an onlooker noted, "When Clift's around, there's only room for one Jesus Christ."

Another explanation of Marlon's sympathetic characterization of the Nazi was offered by Shelley Winters: "Actors can't bear to be hated and Marlon is no exception."

Marlon suffered another personal jolt when, in June 1958, his father remarried. Friends felt that Marlon, who revered the memory of his mother (he had a life-size portrait of her), was further upset because his new stepmother was only twenty-eight. Anna Parramore was a widow who apparently preferred older men. Her first husband, who had been killed in an automobile accident, was twenty-two years older than she. Brando wished his father well but friends recall he was "quite cool toward his stepmother."

For years Brando Sr. had been caught up in the confusion of having the same name as his famous son. (Marlon had once suggested to his father that he change his name. Sr. replied, "Look, Bud, I've had it for thirty-five years longer than you have. If there's going to be any changing, you do it.") Now, to further complicate matters, his new wife had the same name as Marlon Jr.'s wife.

While Sr. had newly found marital bliss, Jr. was heading for his first divorce. Ten days before their first wedding anniversary Anna Kashfi announced she was divorcing Marlon Brando. She had, she said, moved out of their house because her husband was never there. "I can no longer take his indifference and his strange way of living."

In Santa Monica, several months later, Miss Kashfi (through her lawyers, for she was in Hawaii at the time) officially sued Marlon for divorce, alleging that he had caused her "grievous mental suffering, distress and injury." Five weeks later she had the divorce papers in hand, granted on testimony that Brando was frequently absent from home. Under the terms of the divorce she received a half-million dollars' property settlement, with

$60,000 to be paid in cash at once and the rest over a ten year period. She retained custody of Christian Devi.

Anna, many years and personal disasters later, looked back bitterly on her marriage. She claimed she knew she didn't love Marlon when she married him but things had gone too far and she had to go through with it.

They had met in 1956. Their courtship, however, continued in the hospital when she became ill with tuberculosis. Brando visited her frequently and was gentle and kind. According to Anna things went best between them when she was ill and helpless.

Anna has said that no sooner were they married than he began dating other women. Even after Anna and Marlon split, his "other women" caused her anguish. She has remembered one occasion when she came home and discovered Brando and "a certain Asian beauty who shall remain nameless" in bed together. "I walked in and there he was making love to a woman in my bedroom and in my bed, and in my own damned house!" When she demanded that the woman leave, the answer from the girl was a lamp thrown in her direction.

Marlon was always lost in his own dream world, lamented Anna, and life with him depended on whatever movie he happened to be making. During *Sayonara*, for example, he behaved in his personal life the way he did on screen, including expectations that Anna assume the role of a sort of real-life geisha girl. During *The Young Lions*, however, Anna complained that he became domineering and difficult. Another complaint she voiced was that Marlon was a hypochondriac.

Brando, meanwhile, was a very busy man. A professional reunion was in the works for him and Tennessee Williams.

Since *A Streetcar Named Desire*, Williams had wanted Brando for the lead in each of his succeeding plays. In the mid-fifties Williams rewrote *Orpheus Descending*. It had been his first full-length play, originally produced in 1939. The play had always been a critical and commercial failure and he kept rewriting and revising it. Now he had rewritten it for Broadway with Brando

75

and Anna Magnani in mind as the stars.

Marlon turned it down. "I can explain very easily why I didn't do 'Orpheus.' There are beautiful things in it, some of Tennessee's best writing, and the Magnani part is great; she stands for something, you can understand her—and she would wipe me off the stage. The character I was supposed to play, this boy, this Val, he never takes a stand. I didn't really know what he was for or against. Well, you can't act a vacuum. And I told Tennessee. So he kept trying. He rewrote it for me, maybe a couple of times. But—well, I had no intention of walking out on any stage with Magnani. Not in that part. They'd have to mop me up. I think—in fact, I'm sure—Tennessee had a fixed association between me and Kowalski. I mean, we're friends and he knows that as a person I am just the opposite of Kowalski, who was everything I'm against—totally insensitive, crude, cruel. But still Tennessee's image of me is confused with the fact that I played that part. So I don't know if he could write for me in a different color range. . . . There aren't any parts for me on the stage. Nobody writes them. . . ."

Although neither Brando nor Magnani did the roles on stage, they were persuaded to make the film version, titled *The Fugitive Kind*. Marlon's fee and percentage deal was expected to net him $1 million. Academy Award winner Joanne Woodward was also starred, in a role considerably beefed up for the film.

However, Brando's feelings about the role of Val, and Magnani's role, remained the same. At first Brando and Magnani were cautious about each other. "When I work with him it is like I work with a strange animal that is ready to pounce," said Magnani. "Yet it is a wonderful experience to see him be so realistic . . . so completely all man. His style is fantastic." According to Brando, "This explosive woman is the type I like to play opposite. She is real. Of course, she is crazy like me and we have our differences. But actors have a way of understanding these things. We forget very quickly."

However, such dissension developed between them that Brando indulged his penchant for sometimes sadistic "joking"

Tennessee Williams described Brando and Magnani working together as the greatest clash of egos ever seen.

to distract and annoy a performer. If the recollections of a certain publicist are to be believed, "To upset Magnani when she was in the throes of a dramatic scene Brando would sometimes threaten to disrobe and make disturbing gestures."

As production progressed, there were other reports of their constantly being at each other's throats. After shooting was completed, when each was asked if he would work with the other again, the replies were direct: "I do not wish to work with him *ever* again," declared Magnani. Brando said: "Only with a rock in my fist."

Tennessee Williams summed it up: "Brando and Magnani engaged in a clash of egos never again equaled."

Ads for the film read: "And Now The Screen Is Struck By Lightning." However, the box office wasn't, although the film received some excellent reviews.

Back in the silent picture days, when Charlie Chaplin, Mary Pickford, and Douglas Fairbanks formed United Artists, industry savants described the event by saying, "The asylum has been taken over by the inmates." That, plus the old vaudeville phrase "You ain't seen nothin' yet!" was inadequate to describe the next couple of chapters of Marlon's life.

Sam Spiegel wanted Brando for *Lawrence of Arabia*. Brando turned it down. Instead he launched his first independent picture *One-Eyed Jacks,* to star himself and be directed by emerging wunderkind Stanley Kubrick. The budget: a respectable $1.8 million.

Kubrick had distinguished himself via several "small" films, notably *The Killing,* a B-picture, and *Paths of Glory.* He had replaced Anthony Mann as director of the big-budgeted *Spartacus.* Kubrick was a brilliant filmmaker who knew exactly what he wanted regarding script and performances. Shortly after production began on *One-Eyed Jacks,* Kubrick resigned. A friend opined, "Marlon, with his two million ideas on how the film should be done, wasn't happy with Kubrick, who had his own very definite ideas. Since Marlon was the producer as well as star, there wasn't much question as to who would get his own way."

Paramount executives had known when they signed Brando that they were in for a "colorful" time. They hadn't anticipated, however, that Brando would take over the direction himself. "I'd much rather not have to do the directing," he said, "but I had no choice." And now, as producer-director-star, he was "a triple threat man."

With, as one Paramount executive phrased it, "Stanislavsky in the saddle," Brando began directing on location in Monterey, California. The first day on the set he threw the script aside and announced, "We're going to improvise." The tremors were felt from Monterey to Hollywood to Paramount's New York executive offices.

Improvise they did, at a cost of $42,000 a day for six months. One day alone 11,000 feet of film were shot, with only 270 feet being used in the finished picture. There were complaints that Brando sat by the seaside for hours, waiting for the waves "to become more dramatic." When the ulcerating backers complained to Brando, he retorted: "I'm shooting a movie, not a schedule."

One associate remembers Brando's directorial technique: "A combination of soft background music and downright bullying."

Asked what he was trying to do in *One-Eyed Jacks*, Brando assumed the role of artistic producer as he explained, "I have the obligation and the opportunity, in a recently discovered impulse, to try to communicate the things I think are important . . . to make a frontal attack on the temple of clichés. Our early day heroes were not brave one hundred percent of the time nor were they good one hundred percent of the time. My role is that of a man who is intuitive and suspicious, proud and searching. He has a touch of the vain and a childish and disproportionate sense of virtue and manly ethics. He is lonely and generally distrustful of human contacts.

"Properly handled, the folklore of the outdoor era con-

Brando as film director. His controversial *One-Eyed Jacks* was both acclaimed and attacked. Marlon was furious at the studio's decision to trim the five-hour running time to two-and-a-half.

tains all the vital ingredients of powerful picture-making."

Meanwhile, the vital resources of Paramount were becoming strained as the budget of *One-Eyed Jacks* escalated to over $5 million with no end in sight.

"It's been trying," said Brando. "The first few days were very difficult, but it improves as we go along. I work fourteen hours a day. Directing by itself is hard enough. But I've found that there are no divisional lines between an actor becoming a director. Things are so subtly interlaced it is hard to know where one begins and the other ends.

"I've directed myself to a large extent in most of the pictures I have been in," he continued. "My most difficult role was Sakini in 'Teahouse of the August Moon.' I don't think I did it well at all. In 'Guys and Dolls' I wanted to effect a frothy farce style, but I'm heavy-footed with high comedy. I liked 'The Young Lions' but I wish I could have done it better. I gave up in the middle of 'The Wild One' because I was discouraged and disgusted. It was depressing and fruitless. I think I liked 'On the Waterfront' and 'Sayonara.'"

Producer Brando had cast old friend Karl Malden as the film's heavy. Ex-girl friend Katy Jurado also received a major role.

While the studio would have preferred a "name" leading lady for additional box-office insurance, Brando had chosen an unknown Mexican actress, twenty-year-old Pina Pellicer. "As in his private life," says an acquaintance who is no longer Marlon's friend, "he didn't want any competition. It was disaster for him opposite Magnani. With Pellicer, we all knew who the audience would be watching."

"I was afraid when I began to work for him," said Miss Pellicer at the time. "I am still afraid when I go on the set, but I try to do the best I can. Mr. Brando is very kind and patient with me. He is that way with everybody. He takes as much time with an extra as he does with the stars, and he is teaching me many things about acting."

Asked his opinion of Brando's directing, Karl Malden replied: "Marlon says he always told everyone how to make a picture. Now he's doing this one exactly the way he wants it done. He's making all the rules and he's taking all the responsibilities. If it's a flop, he'll be the first to say so."

Jacks was Brando's first western and turned out to be one of the goriest films made up to that time. It proved accurate the accounts of producers who said, "If you want Marlon for a movie promise him a scene where he gets severely beaten." In one scene of *Jacks*, Malden smashes Brando's hand to raw meat.

While in the original version the leading lady was killed, Brando had been persuaded to change this ending since it was considered too downbeat. Finally, after more than $6 million and endless hours of anguish, Brando completed *One-Eyed Jacks*. His initial cut of the film ran over five hours.

"He actually was furious when we told him we weren't going to release a five-hour picture," recounts an ex-Paramount executive. " 'Gone With the Wind' was an hour and a quarter shorter than that. From an exhibitor point of view it was impossible to merchandise a movie that long." The film was edited for distribution and Brando was livid.

Jacks, in a two hour–twenty minute version, finally made its debut on March 30, 1961. Critical reaction was mixed. *Time* magazine said that *One-Eyed Jacks* ". . . turns out to be just a big, slick commercial horse opera. The film, to be sure, is meticulously produced, directed, acted and edited, and is often startlingly beautiful to see . . . the big action scenes, in fact, are ingenious and exciting. Brando seems to combine a small boy's infatuation with violence and a dancer's flair for movement. Director Brando, however, comes off much better than Actor Brando, the Method Cowboy, who incessantly mumbles, scratches, blinks, rubs his nose and sulks. In short, Brando plays the same character he always plays, the only character who seems to interest him: Marlon Brando."

Dwight MacDonald, writing in *Esquire,* said: " 'One-Eyed Jacks' is such an egregiously self-indulgent film. The character that Mr. Brando has been playing for some years now has never had such an uncorseted exposition, doubtless because Mr. Brando was here his own director."

Newsweek called it ". . . one of the most intriguing Westerns ever made . . . it is high achievement that its beautiful, unobstructive direction and strong, subtle acting are in perfect harmony from start to finish."

Karl Malden was not wrong in saying that Brando would admit the movie was a flop, if indeed it was. To the horror of Paramount Pictures, Brando called *One-Eyed Jacks* a "potboiler. I think it is quite conventional . . . I took a long time on it . . . six months to shoot. After a while I got an attachment to it. It's like spending two years building a chicken coop. When you're finished you want to feel you've done something with your time.

"It is not an artistic success. I'm a businessman. I'm a captain of industry—nothing less than that. Any pretension I've sometimes had of being artistic is now just a long, chilly hope. 'One-Eyed Jacks' is a product just like—a news item. News makes money, not art. Movies are not art."

When he was asked to comment on Brando's comment, Malden said: "Marlon is a most unconventional guy—he just can't react the way most people would. I think the majority of people will come out saying this is a great movie. So Marlon will say it stinks. If they were to say 'This stinks,' Marlon would be saying 'There are things in this movie you won't find in any other.'"

One of the things Paramount didn't find in the film was a profit. Although *Jacks* made a respectable showing at the box office, the production was simply too costly. Like Judy Garland in *A Star Is Born*, Brando had delivered a film of top quality but at too high a price.

Brando's discovery Pina Pellicer never made another American movie. She was a tragic, troubled young girl who committed suicide in Mexico City a few years later.

Kashfi and young son, Christian Devi Brando

★ 6 ★

"POOR MARLON," sighs a friend about this period in Marlon's life. "He was so unhappy professionally and his personal life was bananas."

Marlon and Kashfi, soon after their divorce, became involved in a bitter custody fight over Christian that would last for twelve years.

In the first custody hearing, back in January of 1960, Brando was awarded twice-a-month visiting rights. The next year, at another custody hearing, it was revealed that in 1960 Brando had married Movita (their relationship had continued on and off since the *Viva Zapata!* days). What's more, she had borne him a son, Miko. Brando had telephoned the high-strung Miss Kashfi from Tahiti to tell her of this second marriage. "I knew sooner or later this marriage I was in for more than a year would be found out. I thought it would be fair, honest and considerate for me to tell her rather than for her to find it out through gossip. I told her what the circumstances of my marriage were and of the little boy I have by that marriage. It was quite a distressing time for both of us."

Distressing wasn't the word. "Anna was fit to be tied," remembers one of her pals. Kashfi was livid over the fact that Marlon wanted to establish a close relationship between his two sons. "He thinks our child and this other child should get together. My answer was that the children should be left out of it completely. This child of Movita's is his own problem and what

85

he does about him is his business." Miss Kashfi retained custody of Christian.

Although Brando had managed to keep it out of the press, his marriage to Movita had been an impulsive move precipitated by her becoming pregnant with his child. Nasty Hollywood rumors buzzed that the *real* reason Marlon married was to avoid about-to-break adverse publicity concerning his close relationship with lifelong buddy Wally Cox. "Bullshit," laughs one of Brando's former girl friends today. "Marlon went through his own 'period of torment' but got over it. He married Movita for the sake of the child."

Before leaving for Tahiti to start work on his next film, which was destined to be an epic in every way, Marlon Brando embarked on a new career: deep involvement in civil rights causes and new role as champion of the underdog. In some cases the underdogs would resent his involvement.

Though Brando's active involvement didn't begin until this time, he had always been concerned. Years ago, producer John C. Wilson sent Brando the script of Noel Coward's *Present Laughter*. Brando returned the script, along with a note: "I have read it. Do you know that millions of people are starving in Europe and Asia?"

On March 29, 1960, the Committee to Defend Martin Luther King and the Struggle for Freedom in the South placed a full-page ad in *The New York Times* which stated, in part: "In Montgomery, Alabama, after students sang 'My Country 'Tis of Thee' on the State Capitol steps, their leaders were expelled from school, and truckloads of police armed with shotguns and teargas ringed the Alabama State College Campus. When the entire student body protested to State authorities by refusing to reregister, their dining hall was padlocked in an attempt to starve them into submission . . . Decent minded Americans cannot help but applaud the creative daring of the students and the quiet heroism of Dr. King . . . we must heed their rising voices—yes— but we must add our own."

Brando was a signer of this ad, along with others including Tony Franciosa, Van Heflin, Nat King Cole, Viveca Lindfors, Nat Hentoff, Elmer Rice, Norman Thomas, and Mrs. Eleanor Roosevelt.

Marlon's newly found dedication to worthy causes did not, however, consume all his time. Though married to Movita his relationship with other women continued. Eurasian actress France Nuyen had entered his life. The young beauty had emerged a Broadway star in *The World of Suzie Wong,* and her agents expected her to become a major name. However, she got sidetracked. Brando's relationship with Miss Nuyen was serious, particularly from her point of view. Their affair ended sadly. She had been signed to re-create her stage role of Suzie Wong in the film version but lost the part because, according to one source, she was at emotional ends and had gained too much weight. Other sources said Miss Nuyen had indeed gained a lot of weight, the reason being she was pregnant. Whatever the reason she was soon out of Marlon's life and their names were never linked again.

Few people realized that Marlon was also deeply involved with lovely Puerto Rican actress Rita Moreno. Their relationship had continued for some time.

Rita Moreno was an incredibly beautiful girl. Looking back on these years she has observed, "I was really a spoiled bitch. I could snap my fingers and any man would do anything I asked of him."

Brando was not one to put up with such an attitude, especially on a permanent basis. Rita was obviously not emotionally mature enough to handle him at the time. (She has since matured magnificently, as a person as well as an actress. Her professional achievements include an Oscar as Best Supporting Actress for *West Side Story.*) Today Rita Moreno has only kind words for Marlon Brando.

However, at the height of their affair, things were frantic.

Like Frank Sinatra, Brando likes women who keep their love affairs with him private. However, Miss Moreno made headlines on April 19, 1961, when she took an overdose of sleeping

The liaison between Marlon and France Nuyen ended unhappily.

Rita Moreno: gorgeous and talented, she attempted a drastic solution to her Marlon problems.

pills at the home of Brando's secretary, Alice Marshak. Miss Marshak took her to Brando's house. He wasn't there but they went inside and called the doctor. The ambulance arrived before Brando, and Miss Moreno was rushed to a nearby hospital in Santa Monica. But it was too late to avoid publicity. The incident was widely reported as an attempted suicide.

It was a particularly bad period for Marlon and women.

However, a new girl was about to enter his life. Like her predecessors she would be an exotic non-American.

Mutiny on the Bounty, with a final budget of $27 million, is not only one of the most expensive motion pictures ever produced. To this day it remains, along with Elizabeth Taylor's *Cleopatra,* one of the most controversial, not because of what ended up on screen but because of what didn't.

"Why," some people ask, "does Hollywood continue to throw good money after bad? When a performer runs up budgets, presents production problems, why do they constantly get other offers?"

The film industry is the most peculiar industry in the world. It is difficult to point to any one factor as the cause of certain disasters. In some cases the performer, or star, may end up with blame for production delays et al. that are actually the fault of the film company's management. However, there are instances where the star definitely is to blame. And there are still other situations where both star and studio are equally at fault.

No one knows how to guarantee a hit at the box office. To be sure there are certain ingredients that are essential—script, director, cast—but in the final analysis a good, i.e., hit picture is the result of an intangible ingredient. However, the myth continues that stars are box office, and the banks that finance films and the companies that produce and distribute them feel that their investment is protected with a star who has a record of hits.

In the early 1960s, Marlon Brando was rated big box office. Despite his growing reputation as difficult to work with, Brando was still first choice of producers. Even though *Fugitive Kind* had flopped, the feeling was that without Brando and Magnani it would have grossed zero.

"At the time of 'Mutiny' it was Marlon, Bill Holden, Cary Grant," remembers a journalist. "Now it's Redford, Streisand, Paul Newman—but then, as now, their agents were always aware of the worth of top stars and demanded huge salaries and percentages." Not to mention script approval, director approval, and, in some instances, cast approval.

Preparations for *Mutiny on the Bounty* began in 1959. It was the brainchild of distinguished producer Aaron Rosenberg, a tall, ex-All American football tackle newly engaged by MGM after a long career at Universal. In Rosenberg's words: "I had never met Brando, but one day director John Sturges suggested that it might be one hell of an idea for me to do a new version of 'Mutiny on the Bounty,' with Brando playing either of the two major roles, Captain Bligh or Fletcher Christian, the ship's officer who led the revolt. When I contacted Brando he turned me down cold. A short time later Brando's agent came to me saying, 'Marlon is interested in the idea again, but he doesn't want to re-do the old picture, which was mostly about the mutiny. He wants to emphasize the period *after* the mutiny when the mutineers settled on Pitcairn Island, a complete paradise, and yet they ended up killing each other off. He wants to get across the message that the way our society is constituted, people can't live without hate even in a paradise.' We arranged a meeting with Brando and myself and Sol Siegel, who was then head of the studio, but the meeting got nowhere. Brando was unimpressed. So I decided to make the picture with someone else, and Eric Ambler was assigned to write the script.

"After Ambler finished the script I decided just as a long shot to send it to Brando to read. He turned it down again, but again his agent said Brando wanted to see me. When we got together Brando kept emphasizing that he'd play the Fletcher Christian part if we'd rewrite the ending to include a long sequence on Pitcairn Island. I finally made a deal with him agreeing to give him consultation rights on that part of the picture. He signed a contract early in 1960 and we agreed to start shooting the picture on October 15, 1960. I then signed Sir Carol Reed, the British director, and I thought we were all set. But when I took Reed to Brando's house to meet him, I got shaky again. Brando spent two hours trying to get us to do a picture about Caryl Chessman, the executed rapist, before I could even get him to discuss 'Mutiny on the Bounty.' "

As the October 15 starting date approached, the project seemed headed for difficulties. Two new writers, William Driskill and Borden Chase, were hired to help Ambler rewrite the script to Brando's satisfaction.

Rosenberg had contracted with a Nova Scotia shipyard to build a $750,000 replica of the original eighteenth century British man-of-war, H.M.S. *Bounty*. The new version would, of course, be outfitted with hidden engines, air-conditioned dressing rooms, camera mounts and so on.

Rosenberg then went to England and signed Trevor Howard for the role of Captain Bligh; Richard Harris as a mutineer; and Hugh Griffith (who had just won an Oscar for *Ben Hur*). All were set to start filming October 15.

Brando accompanied Rosenberg and Carol Reed to Tahiti to cast the Polynesian members of the company. The casting director had chosen sixteen Polynesian girls from whom Brando would select his leading lady. Marlon took each one, one at a time, into a room with him. To test their acting potential he threatened to throw himself out the window and studied their reactions. All of them giggled.

Eventually he chose beautiful young Tarita Teriipaia for the role. Her detractors liked to remind people that before Brando discovered her she was a waitress and dishwasher in a local hotel.

Brando was romantically drawn to the twenty-one-year-old. They began an affair which has lasted, on the usual Brando terms, more than a dozen years. (In 1962 they had a son, Tehotu. It is fascinating to note Brando's ability to keep certain aspects of his private life secret. Knowledge of this son's existence was not made public until the boy was two years old.)

As the starting date for *Mutiny* grew closer, the script was still not acceptable to Brando. The writers began another version of the Pitcairn Island ending.

Meanwhile, the producer encountered problems with the new *Bounty*. Blizzards had delayed delivery of the necessary lumber for the hull of the ship, and when October 15 arrived

The magnificent Tarita, mother of a Brando son and daughter. She met Marlon at the time of *Mutiny on the Bounty*.

there was no *Bounty*. Even if it had been ready there was no shooting script. There were, however, eighty-nine cast and crew members on salary as of October 15. Brando's deal called for $500,000 as an advance against 10 percent of the gross plus $5,000 a day overtime for each day the film ran over schedule (he eventually collected $750,000 in overtime).

When the *Bounty* was finally completed—two months late—it sailed from Nova Scotia to Tahiti. The trip was appropriately eventful. There were two shipboard fires en route and even the experienced Nova Scotian crew suffered acute seasickness as the ship rolled tremendously. This was due to the special riggings for cameras and other equipment which made the ship top-heavy.

Cast and crew flew to Tahiti to meet the *Bounty*, and production finally began on December 4. Meanwhile, writer Charles Lederer had been hired to replace the first three writers. There was still an incomplete script and it was a daily chore to keep ahead of the shooting schedule. There was no doubt now in the minds of MGM executives that the film would run well over budget. Filming was estimated to be costing $55,000 a day.

Suddenly Brando "threw a curve." After several weeks of shooting he decided he shouldn't play Fletcher Christian after all, but another character—John Adams, the seaman who's the sole survivor of the mutiny. "I felt sorry for the MGM people," says an ex-*Mutiny* member today. "They had asked for trouble by giving in to Brando every step of the way, but they didn't expect anything like his demand to switch roles." Transpacific telephones buzzed, executives gulped more pills, and the idea was vetoed. Brando went back to work as Fletcher Christian— "but unhappily."

And unhappily for all concerned, the company then encountered the Tahitian rainy season. Everyone was brought back to Hollywood. Carol Reed resigned, aware of the insoluble problems which lay ahead. He was paid in full. He was replaced by sixty-six-year-old Hollywood veteran Lewis Milestone, director of, among other respected films, the classic *All Quiet on the Western Front*.

In Milestone's words: "When I came to 'Mutiny on the Bounty'. . . I felt it would be quite an easy assignment because they'd been on it for months and there surely couldn't be much more to do. To my dismay, I discovered that all they'd done was a seven-minute scene . . . in which Trevor Howard issues instructions about obtaining island breadfruit."

"This is when it really all began to fall apart," an observer recalls. There are conflicting reports of ensuing events. "In February Milestone began shooting indoor scenes at the MGM studios," says one source. "Within an hour he and Brando weren't speaking. Milestone was a director from the old school—that is, tell the actor what to do and start the cameras rolling. Brando, on the other hand, utilized the endless discussion method, whereby writer, director and actor work together to 'attain the proper mood,' then set up the camera to 'catch the actor's genius in flight.' When Milestone would tell Brando 'do so-and-so,' Brando's reply would be: 'Why?' Milestone wouldn't answer."

"The crew had bets going that the film would be in production for five years," remembers a gaffer.

Milestone tells it this way: "During the first two weeks on the film Brando behaved himself and I got a lot of stuff done—especially with sequences like the arrival in Tahiti, when I could work with the British actors. I got on beautifully with Trevor Howard, Richard Harris, and the others; they were real human beings and I had a lot of fun. I've remained very good friends with Richard Harris.

"Then the trouble started. I would say that what went basically wrong with 'Mutiny on the Bounty' was that the producer made a number of promises to Marlon Brando which he subsequently couldn't keep. It was an impossible situation because, right or wrong, the man simply took charge of everything. You had the option of sitting and watching him or turning your back on him. Neither the producers nor I could do anything about it."

The war was on. Brando told his aides, agents, and friends that Milestone wasn't going to be satisfactory. Milestone remembered, "Charlie Lederer, the writer on the picture who had recommended me to be director, came to me and said, 'You're working too fast. You better slow down a little.' I said to Charlie, 'Of course I'm working fast. Don't you think enough time has been wasted on this picture already?' Charlie said, 'Yes, but Brando says you're not really interested in the picture and you're speeding things up because you're just trying to get it over with as soon as possible.' I said to myself, 'Aha, it looks as if we're in for a rocky voyage.'"

Milestone has remembered that, when Lederer brought the day's script on the set in the morning, "they would go into Marlon Brando's dressing room and lock themselves up there till lunchtime. I don't know what went on. I never went in there.

"After lunch, they came out. By then it was about two-thirty and we hadn't shot a scene. You had the option of shooting it, but, since Marlon was going to supervise it anyway, I waited until someone yelled 'Camera!' and went off to sit down somewhere and read the paper."

Milestone also commented, "The next thing I knew, Aaron Rosenberg was on the set every day, and Brando was arguing with him about every scene instead of with me, and then they'd call Charlie Lederer and they'd both argue with him. Sometimes they'd argue over one line for hours before a camera would turn. I later discovered that they had decided on a complete democracy in making their decisions: Brando had one full vote and Rosenberg and Lederer each had a half vote. All I can say is, that's a hell of a way to make a picture. The arguments went on until His Highness had won either Rosenberg or Lederer over to his side. Very often I'd take a nap until they informed me His Highness was ready to submit to my cameras. It was harrowing for me, but in terms of the extra sleep I got, quite restful."

At the end of March the group returned to Tahiti to continue outdoor shooting. Brando and Milestone were hardly speaking. A crew member relates: "Brando was really living it up. He had a great villa—lots of Polynesian girls and men around. He played the drums in their local celebrations and loved to take the dames dancing in the local night spots. He didn't seem to give a damn. He'd come in the morning all red-eyed."

According to several sources Brando arrived at morning calls unprepared. According to statements by Lewis Milestone, the actor rarely knew his lines and would require up to thirty takes for a single scene. At other times he used cue or "idiot" cards.

Four months later the cast and crew were still in Tahiti. Milestone felt by this time that "it wasn't a movie production; it was a debating society. Brando would discuss for four hours, then we'd shoot for an hour to get in a two-minute scene because he'd be mumbling or blowing his lines. By now I wasn't even directing Brando—just the other members of the cast. He was directing himself and ignoring everyone else. It was as if we were making two different pictures. But I was having trouble not only with his private mutiny; he had rallied to his side every punk extra who claimed he was a Method actor. If I raised my voice to one of them, Brando would complain to Rosenberg. It got so bad that one 18-year-old punk walked off the set when I refused to reshoot an entire scene in which he 'emotionally felt' his performance was not quite right. I said, 'OK, walk. But don't come back.' Like his master, he sulked for a while—but he came back."

On another occasion Milestone noted, "I've been in this business for forty years, and I've never seen anything like it. Did you ever hear of an actor who put plugs in his ears so he couldn't listen to the director or the other actors? That's what Brando did. Whenever I'd try to direct him in a scene, he'd say, 'Are you telling me, or are you asking my advice?'

"Instead of boarding the 'Bounty' at the dock in Tahiti with the rest of us every morning, Brando insisted on a speedboat to take him out to the ship while we were at sea. Three weeks before we were to leave Tahiti he decided to move from the house we had rented for him to an abandoned villa nearly fifty kilometres away. It cost us more than $6000 to make it habitable for him for the week or two he lived in it. That's the way it was for the many months we were shooting."

Charles Lederer had written eleven versions of the Pitcairn Island sequence. He and Rosenberg agreed on the eleventh and brought it to Brando. The star burned. "This isn't what I asked for! It doesn't show man's inhumanity to man. I wanted to draw a parallel with what is going on in Africa today."

The producer and writer stood firm and when Brando suggested he could write a better ending for the film Rosenberg gave his OK. Two and a half weeks later Brando came forward with his version which had Fletcher Christian sitting in a cave contemplating society's ills while his shipmates pillaged, murdered, and raped on Pitcairn Island. "What he'd done," recalls an observer, "was write himself *out* of the entire last part of the picture."

When Rosenberg rejected Marlon's script and insisted on shooting Lederer's, Brando retorted: "You're making the biggest mistake since the picture started. OK. This is what you want; this is what you're going to get. I'll just do anything I'm told."

One of those closely connected with the film sums it up: "For the next five weeks he just went through the motions. When he was supposed to slug Richard Harris in one scene he sort of swishily smacked him. After a few takes Harris began dancing with him then stormed off and shouted 'When you're ready to work—call me.'"

During this period Brando and Rosenberg hardly spoke. The final sequence cost $2 million to shoot and none of it was usable. Even Rosenberg referred to this period as "six weeks of hell."

An additional problem: During the eleven months of shooting Brando's weight had soared from 170 to 210 pounds. Special lighting and makeup techniques had to be employed to offset this so that "he wouldn't look like Stan Laurel at the beginning of the picture and Oliver Hardy at the end."

Months later Rosenberg was back in Hollywood conferring with MGM executives as to what to do about *Mutiny*. Brando turned up and asked to see a rough cut of the film. Afterward he went to the producer's office: "You know that's a pretty damn good picture—but the ending's no good." Rosenberg stared in amazement and replied, "You're telling *me!*" Marlon then suggested they try a new ending and agreed to waive his $25,000 a week overtime salary for two weeks to do it.

Rosenberg met with Lederer and they called in Ben Hecht to help with a new ending. Milestone saw the script and refused to shoot it. The producer begged him to stick it out for "just two more weeks."

"Fine," Milestone agreed, "but I won't go near the camera—or Brando."

Milestone sat in his dressing room reading magazines while the final scenes were filmed with no visible director behind the camera. All instructions, of course, were from Brando and a nervous Rosenberg standing in the wings. "It was eerie," says Richard Harris, "like seeing a ghost ship with no one at the helm."

According to Milestone, when the picture was completed Brando came to see him, "wanting to know why—as he put it— I'd treated him so badly.

"'I didn't treat you badly,' I said. 'You *behaved* very badly. You didn't even want to discuss the scenes, you just took over.'"

In any case, the production was finally completed. There had been thirteen months of preparation and eleven months of shooting. During that time, three members of the company had died; a Tahitian girl had been fired from the cast for becoming pregnant, but was rehired long after she had had her baby; another Tahitian actress, the second female lead, married a French soldier and moved to Algeria before they got around to shooting her final scenes. Therefore all her scenes had to be cut from the picture.

According to Milestone, Brando "cost the production at least $6 million and months of extra work. . . . I can only say that the movie industry has come to a sorry state when a thing like this can happen, but maybe this experience will bring our executives to their senses. They deserve what they got when they give a ham actor, a petulant child, complete control of an expensive picture."

In Trevor Howard's opinion, Brando's conduct was "unprofessional and absolutely ridiculous," and Richard Harris

99

summed it up for many when he said: "The whole picture was just a large dreadful nightmare for me, and I'd prefer to forget both as soon as my nerves recover from the ordeal."

Concerning *Mutiny on the Bounty* Brando claimed that the costs that piled up were the result of poor executive operations. "The reason for all the big failures is the same," he said. "No script." When that happens, he explained, the star of the film becomes the target of executives "trying to cover their own tracks . . . executives most of whom have gone into the fog and smog of L.A." Brando also said that after Carol Reed left the production, he himself had been asked several times to take over the direction before Lewis Milestone was finally named as the replacement.

Another controversial aspect of the film concerned Brando's characterization of Fletcher Christian. He portrayed him as a foppish, aristocratic dandy. In the 1935 version Clark Gable had come across as masculine, rugged, and down-to-earth. Some critics praised Brando's early Christian contrasted with the later purposeful officer in charge.

Milestone's opinion of Brando's *Mutiny* performance: "I thought it was horrible. I've only seen him act once, and that was on Broadway in 'A Streetcar Named Desire': a marvelous performance. But he was never an actor before and hasn't been one since."

What was Brando's opinion of *Mutiny*? "'Mutiny On The Bounty' is not looked to as a film which will bring new dynamics, new perceptions to the art of the film . . . there are other obvious, saleable aspects of the movie. People from Hollywood presume to be artists where there is no art form, where there's just a crass attention to plebian needs. Nobody ever admits, 'We're out hustling, we're out scuffling, we're out making money.'"

Everyone's worst fears that *Mutiny* wouldn't earn back its costs were realized, despite surprisingly good reviews. The film was in fact MGM's all-time financial disaster.

All thought Brando's *Mutiny*, closely followed by the

Elizabeth Taylor–Richard Burton $40 million *Cleopatra,* would herald the end of the star system. In the words of an industry savant: "No way."

Brando did not lack for job offers. He signed a multi-picture deal with Universal, now run by his former agent Lew Wasserman, and began work on *The Ugly American.* According to industry sources the deal included Universal's buying Pennebaker Productions for $1 million.

Two legends together in a rare photograph: Marlon and Monroe. Their common denominator was the Actors Studio.

★ 7 ★

MARLON BRANDO has on countless occasions stated his
ambivalent feelings about acting. At this point he said, "I haven't
decided what I want to do. I was swept up in acting before I knew
what I wanted to do with myself. This is regarded as an idio-
syncratic impertinence by many people. They think it's some
subtle pretension. But being a movie actor is such a spectacular
and multicolored flashing thing, it's hard to talk about. Let's say
you have a furrier and for eighteen years he worked on 34th
Street cutting furs. He got praise—even adulation—and business
went up. And his friends told him, 'Abe, that's a beautiful coat.'
But there was a kind of emptiness that bothered him, gnawed at
him, and then he found that the thing he really loved to do was
sail his boat in the summer and catch fish. So he became a fisherman.

"Do you remember when Marilyn Monroe died? Everybody stopped work, and you could see all that day the same
expressions on their faces, the same thoughts, 'How can a girl
with success, fame, youth, money, beauty . . . how could she kill
herself?' Nobody could understand it because those are the things
that everybody wants, and they can't believe that life wasn't
important to Marilyn Monroe or that her life was elsewhere.
People have nothing in the lexicon of their own experience to
know what fabulous success is—they don't know the emptiness
of it . . . I'm successful. I'm the Horatio Alger story. I'm the kid
from the middle income bracket who never finished high school,

who went the route of individualism, and made it. I've done what my country told me to do: 'Go on kid! You can do it! That's what we want you to do! . . .' It's a fraud and a gyp. It's the biggest disappointment."

Brando accepted an offer to appear on television on the David Susskind Show. Commenting on statements and slurs against him in magazines and gossip columns, he said, "I have two children growing up in this community and I think that they deserve protection as do their mothers." He also used this occasion to voice his uneasiness about favors granted to movie stars, without their requesting them, because they are movie stars.

With *The Ugly American,* Brando was hoping to make a significant film. His friend George Englund directed. Some people claim Brando imitates people he admires who are well educated. Since Englund was cultured and well dressed, Brando, during this period, became cultured and well dressed. He assimilated words from Englund's vocabulary and as one observer said, "Marlon is such a great inherent actor he actually *became* George Englund."

Brando went to Bangkok for the opening of *The Ugly American.* He mingled with children in the park and the crowds along the streets, creating a very favorable impression everywhere he went. At the premiere he said, "Every Thai is an ambassador . . . I'm genuinely overwhelmed." When a Thai woman, shaking his hand, asked him what he did for a living, he said, "I make faces."

Brando's sister Jocelyn was also in *The Ugly American,* the result of Brando's doing: "I fixed that. You know, she was one of the many performers in Hollywood who were blackballed by the agents because they had innocently joined some reform organization that later was infiltrated by Communists and found themselves unable to get a job.

"If a producer wanted the services of a player whose name was on one of the blacklists, he'd fix it with an agent, and that was all there was to it. But that was done mainly for the stars

With George Englund, producer-director greatly admired by Brando

and well-known players, while the others were just dropped from the lists of available performers."

The Ugly American had a box-office fate similar to *One-Eyed Jacks*. It was a big grosser but cost too much to make a profit.

In July of 1963 Brando announced that he would take part in a Cambridge, Maryland, integration demonstration, defying a National Guard ban against the demonstrations. He attended "as a private citizen—not a representative of the NAACP, the Civil Liberties Union or any other organization."

He said he would also take part in civil rights protests in Baltimore's Gwynn Oak Amusement Park, noting "Children have civil rights as well as adults. White parents teach children discrimination. If children were left to their own devices, they'd learn to get along together." Hospitalization for an acute kidney inflammation kept him from attending as he had promised.

While in the hospital he was hit with a paternity suit by Marie Cui, a Philippine dancer. She charged that Brando was the father of her daughter, Maya Gabriela Cui Brando, born on February 27, 1963, in Manila. She requested $775 a month child support. (A month later Brando submitted to a blood test and a few days later the court announced that Brando was not the father of the child.)

After being released from the hospital, and against the advice of his personal physician, Dr. Robert J. Kositchek, Brando marched with the blacks in Torrance, California, protesting housing discrimination. In reply to criticism from those who said he was doing it solely for publicity, Brando said, "My answer was that it's not a Negro cause. It's mine as well as everybody else's." He further maintained that integration should be Hollywood's special cause, stating: "There is a lot of muscle represented by the stars, if only because of the money involved. We can do something now or let the situation get away from us and have it end tragically. There is little to be said and a great deal to be done." He also said that if he were arrested and had to go to jail, "then I guess I'll go." Then, a month later, he took part in the now famous August 28 march in Washington, D.C.

Marlon at a Civil Rights march

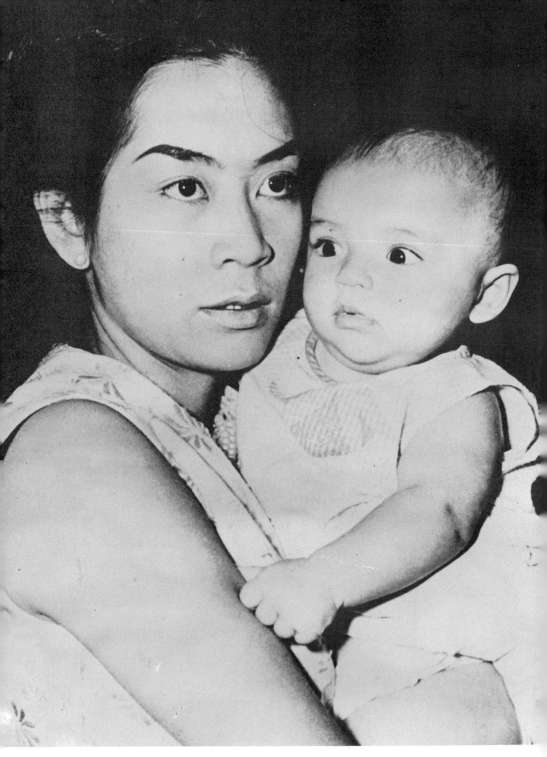

Marie Cui holding the baby she claims was fathered by Marlon Brando

Political columnist James Wechsler wrote an entire column on Brando's involvement in civil rights, noting: "It is a paradox of American politics that, at this critical juncture in the rights conflict, what so celebrated a movie figure does may be more important than what Hubert Humphrey says . . ."

Wechsler concluded, "There are few people with whom I have conversed who seem to know—and care—as much as Brando does about the quest for human dignity in which we are now engaged."

Early in 1964 Brando was revealing his concern about the plight of the American Indians. He went to Washington, D.C., to meet with representatives of the National Congress of American Indians, pointing out that "most people in this country don't know that United States treaties with the American Indian have been broken. They don't know the Indian has been blackmailed into keeping quiet.

"The Bureau of Indian Affairs of the Interior Department has followed a nearly consistent policy to obliterate the Indians. The bureau hit its depths during President Eisenhower's Administration. There was a slight upswing during the Kennedy Administration.

"The Indian has five more years to win a battle of understanding, or he faces extinction.

"People say that Indians are uneducated. Indians are overeducated. They are overeducated in suffering and denial."

At this time he also announced plans to produce and act in "a movie that would tell the story of the misery of the American Indian today." However, because of the nature of their culture, the Indians weren't as receptive to his help as the Blacks had been. One major problem was the lack of unity among the Indian tribes themselves.

Brando became involved in another civic concern. He dined with Jacqueline Kennedy and her sister to discuss plans for a benefit to raise money for the planned Kennedy Center of Performing Arts.

He went to Washington, D.C., to have conversations

with Senator Everett Dirksen about the "public accommodations" provision of proposed civil rights legislation. Reluctant to discuss the details of their conversations, Brando would only say: "I went to Washington trying to play the role of Mr. Citizen, as if I were a dentist from Duluth.

"I did it as a matter of personal conscience—I had to do it, but I don't want to seem to be standing on a soap-box. I regard my conversations with Mr. Dirksen as private ones, but I did want him to know that a lot of us will praise him if he helps get the bill through."

About this time Brando was also engaged in and leading a movement to get Hollywood stars to sign contracts that would include a provision that would prevent the showing of any of their films in any segregated theatre. The idea, originally proposed by a member of CORE, was enthusiastically adopted by Brando.

However, Marlon was forced to turn his attention to personal problems when on December 7, 1964, his son Christian, now six, called police and said his mother was ill. Anna was treated for a possible overdose of "medicine" and also arrested by the police on an assault charge when she resisted their intrusion. Two days later Brando was given temporary custody of Christian.

Two months later, he was given custody of the child on the condition that Christian live with Marlon's sister Frances, now Mrs. Richard Loving, at her home in Mundelein, Illinois. At this hearing Brando was totally frank about his domestic situations. It was at this time that he revealed the existence of his then two-year-old boy Tehotu. He also disclosed that he was separated from Movita, who was living with their son Miko in Mexico, and stated that he hadn't lived with Movita nor had sex relations with her "since the baby was conceived." Why hadn't he divorced Movita? "There has been ample stress these last few years so I thought it best, for Christian's sake, not to stir waters already muddy."

Miss Kashfi testified that she had objected when Brando, several months earlier, had wanted Christian and Tehotu to play together at his home. "It's very disturbing with illegitimate children and mistresses," she declared. Although Anna was placed on six months' probation by the court, victory was eventually hers when later that year the court awarded her custody of Christian.

What wasn't revealed was that Brando had no reason to rush into a divorce from Movita since his relationship with Tarita didn't require marriage.

A few years later, when he finally decided to legally divorce Movita, it became a messy affair. At that time Movita and their son occupied Brando's beautiful mansion on Coldwater Canyon Drive in Beverly Hills. Observers on the scene recall how she had turned the place into a Mexican hacienda complete with live chickens running through the kitchen. The story goes that after the Brando-Movita relationship soured, Movita turned to other men, angering Brando. He finally sold the house to producer Zev Bufman. When Bufman tried to take possession, Movita refused to move, claiming the house was rightfully hers. She wouldn't budge and eventually holed herself up in an upstairs bedroom and had to be forcibly evicted by the authorities.

Marlon's next picture was a Rock Hudson–type comedy teaming him with David Niven and Shirley Jones. David Niven found that Brando, "contrary to what I had heard, was easy, sympathetic and generous to work with." On one occasion during shooting back in '63 Marlon was instrumental in enabling Niven to attend a surprise birthday party for President John F. Kennedy at the White House. At first the producer of *Bedtime Story*, described by Niven as "a staunch Republican," didn't see the necessity of arranging the shooting schedule so Niven could leave early on a Friday night. Brando, "a super Democrat," saw things differently "and the matter was quickly arranged."

Although produced and written by comedy expert Stanley Shapiro, the man responsible for the Rock Hudson–Doris Day successes, the results of *Bedtime Story* were considerably less profitable.

Making *Morituri* at Avalon on Santa Catalina Island in California, Brando was candid about why he was doing the film. "Sometimes, I find I need money. It is like a car and the oil dipstick. You look at it once in a while and find you need oil. Well, every so often I look at my financial condition and find I need money, so I do a good-paying picture. I have three households to support and I pay alimony to two women."

Commenting on the location, Brando said: "This location is like a vacation. It's kind of dull here, but very restful. Yesterday, I was over on the other side of the island. Did you know Shoshone Indians used to live here, and you find many Indian artifacts? I found an old grinding stone."

Asked what he thought about the image some of the public still had of him as a semiliterate animal in a torn T-shirt, he replied: "It's all a fairy tale, of course, but people have a peculiar need to have fairy tales repeated to them. They like to think of certain persons in terms of a particular identity, and they don't want them to play other roles in their minds or their fantasies—they don't want much variation from the original character they endow you with. And, of course, much news reporting helps to perpetuate the myth. News is a commodity, and some items in newspapers and magazines are more saleable—and therefore more lucrative—than others.

"I must say I am impressed by what most people will *believe*. I am always astonished to realize that even the most intelligent, discriminating people will believe almost anything they see in print. I try not to let it bother me. People with enough good sense don't judge until they really know the person, and those who would pre-judge I wouldn't be interested in knowing anyway."

What did he think about the oft-stated possibility that he might have become another Olivier on the stage? He parried the question with his usual ambivalence-about-acting statements. "It may seem peculiar, but I've spent most of my career wondering what I'd really like to do. Of course I've had to make a living, to support children, and wives, but I have a variety of interests—

reading, traveling, meeting people—which have been as important a part of my life as working as an actor. Maybe more so. Perhaps it's hard for people to understand, but acting never has been the dominant factor in my life . . . I have a contract to finish some pictures for Universal, and some other projects in mind. After that—in six or seven years—who knows? I feel as though I have to come to the end of the line somewhere. I just don't picture myself going on much further than that. I'll have to do something —one always has to do something, but I don't know if it will be acting."

In July of '65 Brando suffered another tragedy—the death of his father. Brando Sr. had been the force behind Pennebaker Productions. Under his reign the company had produced such pictures as *Shake Hands with the Devil*, with James Cagney; *The Wild Seed* with Brando-Dean look-alike Michael Parks; *Paris Blues* with Paul Newman, Joanne Woodward, and Sidney Poitier; and *The Naked Edge*, Gary Cooper's last picture.

"What financial security Marlon has today he owes to his father," notes a business associate. "He was a conservative but shrewd businessman. Marlon missed him."

ALTHOUGH HIS FILMS were no longer box-office successes
Marlon was always in demand since each producer felt that his
production would be the one to reignite the Brando magic. In the
late 1960s Marlon chose to work more feverishly than ever.

On the Waterfront producer Sam Spiegel signed him to
star in the multimillion dollar *The Chase,* a heavy "topical" drama
set in the South. The all-star cast included Jane Fonda, Angie
Dickinson, Janice Rule, James Fox, E. G. Marshall, and an exciting "new find," Robert Redford. Arthur Penn was the director
and Lillian Hellman wrote the script, her first in many years.
(However, Horton Foote was called in to modify the Hellman
script, much to her displeasure.)

"Marlon was a tortured man in the early days and he
was great on screen," reminisced Spiegel. "When he ceased being
tortured he had to pseudotorture himself in order to function."
Marlon has corroborated this theory. "You have to upset yourself.
Unless you do, you cannot act. And there comes a time in one's
life when you don't want to do it anymore. You know a scene
is coming where you'll have to cry and scream and all those
things, and it's always bothering you, always eating away at you
. . . and you can't just walk through it . . . it would be really
disrespectful not to try to do your best."

As always, Brando had second thoughts about the interpretation of his role and often proposed new ideas to the director.
"We had a good interchange of ideas," said Penn. "Marlon told

On the set with Martha Hyer and Janice Rule

me at the onset that he would present his ideas and that if I
didn't like them I should tell him so." Penn added that during
production most of Marlon's ideas had been "excellent." *The
Chase* included the obligatory beat-up scene.

The film bombed.

Back at Universal hopes were high when Brando agreed
to star for "hot" young British director Sidney Furie, fresh from
the success of *The Ipcress File,* in a western drama, *The Appaloosa.* The script was top-drawer but there were problems
ahead. Furie didn't enjoy working with Brando. "He loves chaos,"
the director observed on one occasion. "You simply can't get past
'B' in a conversation with Brando and you can't get him to discuss
a script rationally."

Although *Bedtime Story* producer-writer Stanley Shapiro had found Brando cooperative and intelligent, Furie claimed:

"He's disorganized. No discipline at all. A procrastinator. One little scene that should have taken us a few hours to film took ten days. Every day he had another complaint—his tummy ached, his head ached—you should have heard the moans. What a performance! Then he'd be searching for his lines. Anything to procrastinate."

According to printed reports Brando and Furie had fights on the set. Brando would shout, "What the hell do you know?" The director, embarrassed in front of the crew, would shout back: "You may be the star but you're full of crap."

The film was another box-office disappointment. A couple of years later Furie and Brando ran into each other in London. Brando was surprisingly friendly: "It takes me a long time to get to know people," he told Furie. "I thought you were a phony, a liar, a dirty double-crosser. I discovered you've got the great visual sense of good directors. Let's do another film."

"Never!" Furie told friends. "Never."

In 1966, Marlon was supposed to take part in planned marches in Mississippi. Sammy Davis, Jr., announced that Brando, Burt Lancaster, and he would go to Mississippi to demonstrate to "Negroes there that other Negroes and white people aren't afraid to give them spiritual and moral support to get out and vote." Of Brando Davis said, "Marlon's a standup guy who has the courage of his convictions. I'm just sorry more Hollywood people aren't able to join us."

Marlon's career sorely needed a shot in the arm and it seemed the coup of the cinema decade when Charlie Chaplin, for his eagerly awaited comeback picture, *A Countess from Hong Kong*, chose Brando and Sophia Loren as the stars.

Countess was a first in several respects: it was Chaplin's first film in color, the first time he directed established stars, and the first time in decades that he worked for a company not his own.

Everyone felt this would be it, the picture that would

With equally socially conscious confrere, Shirley MacLaine

not only bring Chaplin back into the ranks of active filmmakers but which would restore Brando's prestige to its former heights.

Chaplin had toyed with the idea of *Countess* for thirty years and now he felt he had finally found someone equal to himself to play the lead.

Brando accepted the role, which was sought after by every major star in the business (including the industry's hottest box-office attraction of the day, Sean Connery), without ever having seen the script. "I would have acted in the telephone book, with him directing."

The cast anticipated the thrill of working with the Master. Initially industryites were dubious when Brando was absent the first three days of shooting, the explanation being he had suffered an acute appendicitis attack. However, after he re-covered, Brando was on time every day, lines learned, makeup on.

Lewis Milestone was a wild, avant-garde director compared to Chaplin. Chaplin expected Brando to play the role in a style totally unlike anything he'd ever done. "In the next few days I thought I had gone raving mad and it was impossible," said Brando. "I can't do fades and triple-takes and things like that and I was wanting to go to Charlie to say, 'I'm afraid we've both made a horrible mistake.' But then it all started to work out. With Charlie it's chess, it's chess at ninety mph."

But the honeymoon was shortly over. When Marlon began asking questions about why he should do such and such, Chaplin wasted no time in "explaining" that he was seventy-seven years old and had been in the business a long time and when he told Marlon to do something he should do it or leave immediately and he'd replace him. Marlon got the message.

Both Brando and Sophia watched as Charlie acted out *exactly* how he wanted the roles played. If they had started out enthusiastically, their enthusiasm was short-lived.

During production Marlon remarked, "My style of act-ing has always been sort of, well, *roomy*. This is different. It's a mosaic, mosaic acting, with each tiny piece honed and polished and put in place."

During lunch breaks Brando would go to his trailer dressing room to sleep. In the evenings or on weekends he would screen old Chaplin films in his apartment.

On other pictures, with directors he worked well with, Marlon was, as he has said, "a three-take man" when things were going right. But Chaplin insisted on endlessly reshooting scenes until he felt they were perfect. On one scene, they were up to Take 20 by the end of the day. Brando, who had been on his feet most of the time, wasn't amused. Even Sophia, not in the scene, was anxious to get home.

Countess was the first time since the movie version of *Streetcar* that Marlon was working with a leading lady who was as big a star as he. The practical joker in Brando surfaced when during a love scene with Sophia he looked up her nose and remarked, "You have black hair in your nostrils." Sophia was understandably cool to Marlon from that point on.

Old friend Bob Condon came to visit Brando on the set. Marlon introduced him to Chaplin: "This is an old, old pal from New York—why once in a moment of extreme need he really came through."

"Oh, really," answered Chaplin politely.

"Yeah," said Marlon. "He boosted me over the top of a pay toilet door."

Many noted that Brando, as always, went out of his way to be polite and charming to "little" people he came in con-

Sophia Loren, Sydney Chaplin, Brando on the *Countess from Hong Kong* set in London. By film's end Loren and Marlon were less than good friends.

tact with at the studio during the course of his working day. He was patient beyond the call of duty with the man assigned to wardrobe fittings and other personnel who performed the countless tasks which add up to a complete motion picture.

In early 1967, *Countess* premiered in London. Days before the glittering event Marlon checked into the chic Buxted Park reducing spa in Sussex, England, to lose ten pounds. He looked terrific at the premiere and charmed everyone in sight. At the elegant postpremiere party, many of Chaplin's titled old friends from London society filled the room. The party was a smashing success. Universal-MCA Chairman of the Board Jules Stein was heard to remark, "Too bad we can't release the party instead of the picture."

Brando, who had regarded Chaplin with awe, was completely disenchanted when he saw *Countess*. Afterward, a columnist wrote that Marlon mimicked Chaplin and in turn Chaplin did exquisitely accurate imitations of Brando. In any event, despite an avalanche of worldwide publicity, the film failed, both artistically and commercially.

During these years Marlon shuttled back and forth between America, Europe, and his new love, Tahiti, where to this day he maintains a home with Tarita. He has bought a group of uninhabited islands near Tahiti, going there as frequently as possible and living a back-to-nature *Swiss Family Robinson*–type of existence—"a boyhood dream made real," notes a journalist.

Brando loves these islands. "Being in Tahiti gives me a sense of the one-to-one ratio of things. You have the coconut in the tree, the fish in the water, and if you want something to eat, you somehow have to get it."

Marlon remains close to his three sons. He has succeeded in keeping the children out of the public eye, insisting they be reared as "normally" as possible.

Once again cineasts anticipated a thrilling performance from Brando when he agreed to star opposite Elizabeth Taylor in *Reflections in a Golden Eye*. The role was originally set for

Montgomery Clift. Miss Taylor had agreed to star in the project only if Clift was her costar. When he died, it seemed the film would be abandoned but Brando agreed to take over the role. "The appeal to me of a neurotic role like Major Penderton? $750,-000 plus 7½ percent of the gross receipts if we break even. That's the main reason. . . . Then the attraction of a book by Carson McCullers.

"As for the part itself, it's hard for me to be articulate about acting. What can you say about a certain moment or expression? It's like Chaplin chewing a rose and just looking—there at the end of 'City Lights'—or that final cry by Olivier in 'Oedipus Rex.'"

For the first time since *Streetcar* he took second billing. Again he was working with a legendary director, veteran John Huston. With three such distinct personalities, the industry expected fireworks during production. "Brando wasn't used to working with leading ladies who were treated on the same level as he," notes a publicity man. "However, to everyone's surprise, there were no ego problems."

Unfortunately, there were other problems, namely transferring the delicate Carson McCullers story to the screen. Although Brando tried his best in the role of the frustrated, latent homosexual army officer, the film didn't work and was yet another critical and financial disappointment.

Brando's ex-agent Jay Kanter was now head of MCA-Universal's London operation. Marlon agreed to star in a low-budget thriller, *The Night of the Following Day,* to be filmed in Europe. Brando knocked off a lot of weight for his role as the kidnapper.

Actor Richard Boone was signed to costar and direct. Brando's old friend Rita Moreno was given the female lead. Obviously Boone's directorial technique was Marlon's cup of tea. They got along famously and today Boone looks back on the film as a terrific experience.

He calls Brando one of "two of the finest and most honest performers." (His other choice is Patty Duke.) Discussing two specific weeks of directing Brando he said, "For twelve days the scoreboard lighted up." Brando and Duke have what Boone describes as "a flat honesty. They don't care where the dressing-room is or whether they have a car to drive them on the lot. With them it's 'Where's the work?' That's what I like."

Brando was good friends with French producer Christian Marquand, who conceived the idea of doing *Candy* as a film. Marquand convinced Brando to take the role of the guru, and Marlon in turn convinced Richard Burton to do a role. With Brando and Burton, Marquand was able to line up the rest of the all-star cast for a production slated to further the careers of no one connected with it.

The Night of the Following Day was tense and effective. Many of the scenes had the look of improvisation. But, except for *Time* magazine, critical reaction was negative and the film was overlooked by the public.

Brando's interest in civil rights remained intense. In April of 1968 he marched in a funeral procession for slain Black Panther leader Bobby James Hutton, killed by police in predominantly black West Oakland after emerging from a barricade on a police order.[*] The police claimed they fired after someone saw a gun in Hutton's hand. At the memorial service which followed, Brando addressed the crowd: "You've been listening four hundred years to white people and they haven't done a thing . . . I'm going to begin right now—informing white people what they don't know. The reverend said you 'can't cool it if you ain't dug it.' I've got a lot to learn."

Later, because of comments he made on a television show about the slaying of Hutton, Brando was slapped with a $25 million defamation suit by the police. The suit was eventually and quietly dismissed.

Around this time Marlon made news by accepting, then refusing the starring role in Elia Kazan's screen version of his best-selling novel *The Arrangement*. Brando said he wouldn't do

[*] The police were later exonerated.

Marlon at a sit-in. He knows his presence will attract attention and, when it's for a worthy cause, welcomes it.

Marlon at the funeral of Black Panther leader Bobby James Hutton (1968)

the film because he wanted to devote more time to working on social problems. He was still talking about the picture he planned about the plight of the American Indian.

While many continued to feel that Brando's involvement in civil rights was that of a dilettante, those close to him know that he's a man of honest convictions who quietly devotes not only his time and energy but also money to the causes he believes in. In addition Brando manages to elicit donations from wealthy acquaintances. When Brando was congratulated on convincing a noted millionaire to invest "in one of Marlon's many save-the-world projects," Brando, with characteristic humor, replied: "Wasn't hard. All I had to do was rub his hump with yak butter, and suck on his earlobes a little."

Marlon had been more than dissatisfied with his recent films, although some critics still defended him, calling him "the most exciting actor in motion pictures." They blamed Brando's failures on the material. He, they said, gave the impression of rising above the material. Brando was so original and had been so copied that he had been driven to self-parody.

The Arrangement would have reunited Marlon with mentor Kazan. Speculation at the time was that Brando was not willing to risk the possible ultimate disappointment of an unfulfilling Kazan-Brando project.

Brando also turned down the starring role in *Butch Cassidy and the Sundance Kid* but signed to star for Italian director Gillo Pontecorvo, who had been lauded for "a masterpiece of moviemaking, 'The Battle of Algiers.'" The new film, originally titled *Quemada*, when eventually released in the U.S. was retitled *Burn!* The film had more than its share of problems resulting from clashes between Brando and Pontecorvo, and production went over budget. At one point the animosity between director and star was so intense that Brando confided to a friend that he'd like to strangle Pontecorvo.

Throughout the sixties Brando had attempted to combine moviemaking with social commitment. However he was still a man torn by personal conflicts and paradoxes. One critic summed it up: ". . . there is a curious complexity about the man. Socially committed, he seeks out roles—as in 'The Ugly American' and 'The Chase'—that hold a significance for our times. But once having accepted them, the actor takes over. Like Sinatra, he is aware that his star presence is enough to insure the production of the picture. But where Sinatra is delighted to fly away at the first opportunity, Brando demands his close-ups, his social statements, his martyrdom. I have never seen Brando give a more flaccid, dull performance than the one he offers as Sir William Walker, a nineteenth century British prototype of a CIA agent in Gillo Pontecorvo's 'Burn.' He is certainly aware of the timely cross-references to be extrapolated from this tale of an English agent who foments a black revolution in a Portuguese colony in order to bring it under British rule. At the same time, he is also aware of his star prerogatives."

Burn! too proved a failure at the box office.

Marlon was able to escape the pressures of his profession. He returned to Tahiti. Brando and Tarita had another child, Marlon's first daughter, whom they named Tarita, in 1970. Rumor had it that he wanted to marry Tarita legally according to laws of Western Culture, but she was—and remains—perfectly content to maintain their relationship as it is. According to Tahitian custom there is no need for them to further cement their ties.

Young actor Edward Albert was in Tahiti, living only a few doors away from Brando. On a recent occasion Albert visited him. He knocked on Brando's door, but there was no answer. He went to the kitchen window and spotted Marlon, busy cooking. Albert knocked on the window. Brando saw him and smiled. "We talked a lot that day," remembered Albert, "about his children and about all I'd been doing since he last saw me."

Albert noted that a woman was present, washing clothes. Outside in the rain, children were playing. "At least one of them —a boy with dark skin and blonde hair—was Brando's," he observed.

The young actor and Marlon spoke of the problems of "being a public personality, about how important it is to keep your own life—your own center—within yourself."

Albert is of the opinion that nobody really *knows* Brando, "but I have the feeling that he believes somewhere along the line he missed something he could have done, something he could have been. This sounds strange, but it's as if somebody had put an angel inside of him, and he's aware of it, and it's more than he can *contain*. I walked away from Brando's house that day feeling very sad, very lonely."

Brando continued to travel and work. He went to England to film *The Nightcomers*, directed by intense, talented young Britisher Michael Winner. *Nightcomers* was a return for Brando to a character that was at times brutal, sexual, and gentle. Now, twenty years after *Streetcar*, the screen was allowed to be totally frank in its love scenes. There was nudity in *Nightcomers* and one graphic, sadistic "love scene."

However, Marlon was no longer altogether acceptable on screen in the role of a stud. In some scenes he appeared to have a beer belly.

Nightcomers was an independent production and the final film was not picked up by an American distributor for some time. There was no question about it—Brando was, to utilize an old Hollywood phrase, box-office poison.

★ 9 ★

Not since the nationwide search for an actress to play Scarlett O'Hara had there been so much public interest in who would play a particular film role. The part was the title role in the screen version of what has been described as the *Gone With the Wind* of gangster novels, *The Godfather*.

While author Mario Puzo says he had Brando in mind when he wrote the novel, Paramount Pictures executives, headed by then president Stanley Jaffe, nixed Brando as the star. According to Puzo, before he even suggested Brando to Paramount he personally contacted the actor through a mutual friend. Brando called Puzo back, was very cordial but told him he knew he would never get the part unless a major director pushed for him.

At one point Paramount production chief Robert Evans was quoted as saying the entire production would be cast with "nonstars" and sources said if indeed the studio was going to use a "name" for Don Corleone, it would be someone in the proper age bracket like Edward G. Robinson. To Puzo's dismay, even Danny Thomas was mentioned as a possibility.

While *The Godfather* has become *the* phenomenal best seller of recent times, it was an unexpected coup for Paramount when they bought the screen rights, on the basis of reading the book in galley form, for only $35,000 (with a sliding scale that eventually brought the price to the neighborhood of $80,000). Had Puzo waited until after publication, he could have received $1 million for the screen rights.

Since Paramount had recently produced a "gangster picture" which flopped—*The Brotherhood*—they were wary of *Godfather*'s prospects and the project was assigned to then minor producer Albert Ruddy. Francis Ford Coppola, who had directed, among other films, one small-budget hit (*You're a Big Boy Now*) and one big-budget flop (*Finian's Rainbow*), was signed to direct. Puzo was hired to write the screenplay for the modestly budgeted (between $1 and $2 million) production.

Ruddy and Coppola wanted Laurence Olivier for the lead. He was unavailable. Their next choice was Brando, but the studio, for obvious reasons, wasn't anxious to have him: he hadn't had a hit in years and budgets always seemed to mount on Brando's pictures.

Meanwhile, the novel was sent to Brando, who read it in three days. He wanted the role. It was an ironic situation, since for the past two decades it had always been Brando who was sought after by studios. Now, they had something *he* wanted to do.

A long battle ensued between studio forces for Brando and those opposed to casting him. "We got an absolutely violent response," stated Ruddy. So "violent" that for the first time since he had become a star, Marlon Brando tested for a part. Not officially, of course. What he did was to make his own "homemade" test via video tape. He did his makeup and lighting and directed himself in a short scene as an old Italian sipping a cup of espresso and puffing on an Italian cigar. The test was flown to New York, and Paramount executives, not knowing who was testing, viewed it. Robert Evans remarked to Ruddy, "He looks Italian. Fine. But who is it?" Evans was won over and Brando got the part.

There has been much speculation as to financial arrangements. Reports on Brando's salary range from a straight percentage deal to $50,000 plus a percentage to Brando's version: $250,000 plus a percentage. Industryites concur on the $50,000-plus-percentage figure with a ceiling on Brando's ultimate take in the vicinity of $1 million.

The Godfather received a staggering amount of publicity while in production and not only because of interest in the book and Brando. Producer Ruddy made national headlines when he entered into "a deal" with the Italian-American Civil Rights League not to use the words Mafia or Cosa Nostra in the film. What the League didn't know was that the script never utilized the terms in the first place!

The worldwide attention the film garnered during this period, coupled with the burgeoning sales of the novel, caused Paramount to rethink their plans. The film was elevated to major-major status and the budget was upped to $6.2 million. "By this point, 'The Godfather' simply could not turn out to be a hum-drum affair or Paramount's image would suffer," noted Ruddy. "Two weeks into the shooting, the picture had become a crusade."

Filling other roles was a major problem. "The controversy over casting was grueling," said Al Pacino. "I went back for testing three times—a thing like that eats at your dignity. You'd arrive on the set and someone who was there before suddenly wasn't there anymore. I'd ask someone, 'Am I still here?' and he'd say, 'Yeah, Al, you're still here.'"

Pacino won the plum role of Michael, the Godfather's youngest son who eventually takes over the family business. Another key role was that of Sonny, the Godfather's oldest son. Actor Burt Reynolds, whose physical resemblance to the young Marlon Brando was often commented on, felt that the similarity would finally result in a good role for *him*. Reynolds spoke to Ruddy who, a few weeks later, told him: "Sorry, Burt, but Brando doesn't want you in the picture." Ruddy quoted Brando as saying: "No way."

Vic Damone was announced for the part of crooner Johnny Fontane, the character in the book many people thought was modeled after Frank Sinatra. For reasons never made public Damone changed his mind about accepting the role and was replaced by Al Martino. Another casting surprise was singer Morgana King in the nonsinging role of Mama Corleone (Ava Gardner had been mentioned for the role). John Marley, initially considered for the title role, got the part of the Harry Cohn-like movie mogul.

Paramount kept strict security wraps on the production. No photographs of Brando in makeup were released. No interviews were granted. Everything was hush-hush.

There were further arguments about budget and shooting schedules and Coppola was almost fired on three separate occasions. Evans backed him and so did Brando.

For the most part Brando and Coppola got along perfectly and Coppola later revealed, "Everyone advised me to assert myself with him and say, 'Now, Marlon, I'm the director, you just act.' That would have been suicidal." Coppola realized that with Brando one had to be a listener. "I could understand how he got his reputation because his ideas were so bizarre, so apparently crazy . . . yet without exception every one of his crazy ideas I used turned out to be a terrific moment." It was Brando's idea to put an orange peel across his teeth in the scene where he's playing with his grandson. In Coppola's words: "Brando wants to do what you want but he wants people to be honest and not try to manipulate him."

As always, Brando was concerned with the theme of the film as well as the plot. He tried to influence Coppola to present the story as an allegory of corporate America. Marlon's concept of his role reveals that his desire to do the film was connected with his feelings about problems in America: "I don't think the film is about the Mafia at all. I think it is about the corporate mind. In a way, the Mafia is the best example of capitalists we have. Don Corleone is just any ordinary American business magnate who is trying to do the best he can for the group he represents and his family.

"I think the tactics that Don used aren't much different from those General Motors used against Ralph Nader. Unlike some corporate heads, Corleone has an unwavering loyalty for the people that have given support to him and his causes and he takes care of his own. He is a man of deep principle and the natural question arises as to how such a man can countenance the killing of people. But the American Government does the same thing for reasons that are not much different from those of the Mafia. And big business kills us all the time—with cars and cigarettes and pollution—and they do it knowingly."

Brando and Coppola had few run-ins. Marlon was totally cooperative and late only on a few Monday mornings. One Monday Marlon arrived around noon and proceeded to complain to Coppola about an entire scene. "Marlon, you're incredible," said Coppola. "You're late and you hit me with something so I can't get mad at you." Brando laughed and tension passed.

"In actuality," reports a Paramount executive, "instead of causing trouble Brando helped hold the whole thing together. He even worked an extra week without pay and helped the less experienced actors like Martino."

Coppola has remembered that "Marlon even slapped Martino around to get the right reactions so Martino would look good." Al Pacino noted: "I felt that Brando really cared for me personally and that acceptance was a great thing for me."

Brando's sense of humor remained intact. He, James Caan, and Robert Duvall (who was playing Tom Hagen, the Godfather's adopted son) engaged in a "mooning" contest. "Mooning" is described by one who had participated as "a rather sophomoric game of quickly baring your ass to a group of people—usually from a window or in a crowd. The trick is to do it so quickly and inconspicuously that those seeing it must wonder if they've *really* seen it."

Caan considered himself *Godfather's* "mooning" champ. He had even "mooned" in the window of a limousine as he, the cast, and crew were riding down Manhattan's Second Avenue. But Caan later lamented that he lost out to Brando and Duvall, who managed to "moon" in front of the hundreds of extras assembled for the film's wedding sequence.

When *The Godfather* premiered in New York, Brando was unable to attend. "It's a damned shame," laments a Paramount executive. "This was one premiere Brando really wanted to come to. He was all set, too, right up to the last minute."

Christian as he looks today

A personal crisis had arisen.

For several years matters relating to custody of Christian Devi had remained relatively calm. Both parents shared custody until March 1972, when a Mexican newspaper reported that Christian, thirteen, had disappeared and might possibly have been kidnapped while on a fishing trip in Baja California. A spokesman for Brando, however, reported that the child was well and on a scuba diving excursion in Mexico. Meanwhile, Anna Kashfi failed to show up for a custody hearing after she had been arrested on March 8 in El Centro, California, on charges of public drunkenness and having created a disturbance.

Two days later Christian appeared to be all right as he reentered the United States at Calexico, California. At the next custody hearing, two days afterward, a private detective testified that he and a group of Mexican police found Christian in a tent at a fishing camp in Baja California. He said that one of the fishermen told him that the boy's mother had promised him $10,000 to "heist" the boy. Miss Kashfi was not present at the hearing.

The matter was, to say the least, unsettling. For the sake of the child, Brando stayed with him and did not attend the premiere of *The Godfather* in New York on March 14. (The matter of Christian's custody was finally settled on May 8, 1972, when Brando and Miss Kashfi reached an out-of-court agreement in which Brando would get sole custody and Miss Kashfi would get frequent visiting rights.)

When *The Godfather* opened in New York, it—and Brando—were practically unanimously hailed by critics. More importantly, from the first day there were lines around the block at *each* of the five theatres which were playing the movie. More than a box-office success, the film was a phenomenon. Exhibitors upped their admission prices in New York to four dollars. Traffic was blocked on roads from New Jersey into the city. This was typical of the film's popularity throughout the country.

The Godfather has become the highest-grossing motion picture of all time.

Brando asked $500,000, plus 10 percent of the gross, to star in the planned sequel.

Marlon was back on top. He was on the covers of *Life* and *Newsweek*. He was cajoled and paid to do an interview with *Newsweek*. Not directly paid, but Paramount's Robert Evans promised to give $100,000 backing toward the film Brando wished to make about the Plains Indians.

Speaking again of the Indians, Brando said: "Christ Almighty, look at what we did in the name of democracy to the American Indian. We just excised him from the human race. We had 400 treaties with the Indians and we broke every one of them. It just makes me roar with laughter when I hear Nixon or

Westmoreland or any of the rest of them shouting about our commitments to people and how we keep our word when we break it to the Indians every single day, led by this Senator Jackson from Washington State, perhaps the blackest figure in Indian history, who votes against giving the Indians back the lakes and fishing rights that treaties clearly entitle them to."

In addition to talking about the Indians and his new film project (Brando plans to make his film with British director Peter Watkins), Marlon was willing to discuss his approach to acting: "Acting is as old as mankind. We even see it among gorillas, who know how to induce rage and whose physical postures very often determine the reaction of other animals. No, acting wasn't invented with the theatre. We all know all too well how politicians are actors of the first order. That's been demonstrated by their behavior as shown in the Pentagon papers. We should really call all politicians actors. . . .

"We also carry in us the seeds of any character that we might play. We all entertain the full spectrum of human emotions. Acting in general is something most people think they're incapable of but they do it from morning to night. Acting is the guy who returns from some out-of-town wingding with some bimbo and tells his wife, 'Oh, I had a terrible time.' He's acting. In fact, the subtlest acting I've ever seen in my life is by ordinary people trying to show that they feel something that they don't or trying to hide something that they don't or trying to hide something. It's something everyone learns at an early age. I think anybody can act. I never really understand why anybody would want to use actors. I guess they're used because they've become household pets."

Brando was candid about his attitude toward work. "Most movies are rehearsals. They're improvisations. You're supposed to appear on the set with all your trappings and your doodads in character and you haven't the slightest idea of who you are and what you're supposed to do and usually, about the last third of the picture, you kinda get the idea of what you're doing. If you were to do the same thing in the theatre, it would be ridiculous. But that doesn't happen in films—you just walk in and do the first scene and the only rehearsal you've had is in your mind when you're sitting in the bathtub or driving down to the post office or something. It's always a guessing game. . . . Sometimes you think you're doing badly and it turns out to be good . . . and sometimes it really does turn out to be pretty awful. It's mostly hunt and poke. You really don't know half the time what you want to do. You make it up as you go along."

Despite what a few dissenting critics thought about his performance as Don Corleone (and the opinion of some fellow actors like John Gielgud who thought his performance was mannered and slowed up the film), there was no doubt that most moviegoers agreed Brando had done a tremendous job. "It's a comeback," enthused many in the industry. Brando pooh-poohs that kind of comment. "I've had good years and bad years and good parts and bad parts and most of it's just crap. Acting has absolutely nothing to do with being successful. Success is some funny American phenomenon that takes place if you can be sold like Humphrey Bogart, Shredded Wheat or Marlon Brando wrist watches. When you don't sell, people don't want to hire you and your stock goes up and down like it does on the stock market."

For the most part Brando's success still hasn't provided him with much personal satisfaction or made him believe in "the American way of life." In his words: "Success has made my life more convenient because I've been able to make some dough and pay my debts and alimony and things like that. But it hasn't given me a sense of joining that great American experiment called democracy. I somehow always feel violated. Everybody in America and most of the world is a hooker of one type or another. I guess it behooves an expensive hooker not to cast aspersions on the cut-rate hookers, but this notion of exploitation is in our culture itself. We learn too quickly the way of hookerism. Personality is merchandised. Charm is merchandised. And you wake up every day to face the mercantile society . . .

"The things that give me satisfaction are personal and have nothing to do with my business."

As always he zealously guards his private life: "My personal feelings, my personal involvements are not the business of the press. I don't want to share them with thousands of people that I've never known and never will know and I don't want to be a pawn."

Journalist Shana Alexander has observed, "To him, interviews are fake: acting is real." With reporters he has known for years and feels comfortable with, like Shana, he will ask *them* questions: "Are you an ectomorph? . . . What kind of underwear do you wear? Who would you have been in the eighteenth century? Did you know you have a twitch under your left eye?"

At interviews he sometimes scowls that "for reasons that are not completely known to me consciously, I cannot reconcile myself to sitting and blabbering to you for public benefit, and money." Marlon regards questions about his private life as "navel-picking, AND SMOKING IT!"

On the heels of *The Godfather* and despite his unfulfilling relationship with Gillo Pontecorvo, Brando decided to work with another noted Italian director, Bernardo Bertolucci (who did *The Conformist*). The new film: *Last Tango in Paris*. Brando looked forward to working in his favorite city.

Although after *The Godfather* producers again wanted Brando—"'The Godfather' made Marlon fashionable again. People are willing to put money in his pictures once more," said Ray Stark—it wasn't a snap for Brando and Bertolucci to get financial backing for *Last Tango in Paris*.

Paramount had been offered the project before they released *The Godfather*. They balked at Brando's demand for a $200,000 salary plus a percentage of the gross and offered him $100,000.

Brando and Bertolucci went to United Artists and the film was brought in for a budget of $1.1 million.

The two leading roles for *Last Tango* were originally slated for Jean-Louis Trintignant and Dominique Sanda. They were unavailable so Bertolucci cast Maria Schneider, a newcomer, and hoped to sign Brando.

Brando had admired Bertolucci's *The Conformist* and

expressed interest in working with him. They arranged to meet in Paris.

"For the first 15 minutes he didn't say a word," recalled Bertolucci, "he only looked at me. Then he asked me to talk about *him*. I was very embarrassed, but I got around it by talking about the character I had in mind for the film. He listened carefully and then said yes right away, without asking to read the script."

Bertolucci then came to Hollywood and spent two weeks with Brando, "getting acquainted."

Back in Paris there was no problem between director and star. And Brando began his relationship with costar Schneider by leading her to a nearby bar, where he told her, "We're going to go through quite a lot together, so let's not talk. Just look me in the eye as hard as you can."

He sent her flowers the next day and "from then on, he was like a daddy."

Naturally, gossip circulated that he was being more than "a daddy," and that the very graphic, sexual scenes in the film were not "simulated." Maria discounted this. "We were never screwing on stage. I never felt any sexual attraction for him, though my friends all told me I should. But he's almost 50, you know," she noted, as she ran her hand down her body to her stomach—". . . he's only beautiful to here."

However, Maria was grateful for his professional advice. She said she was "full of his vibrations. That heavy, very slow movement. His ability to size up a scene in an instant and then do it perfectly naturally. In the movie, his character takes that girl and teaches her a lot of things, makes her stretch, makes her explode. That's what he did to me as an actress."

Marlon did provide director Bertolucci with one disconcerting note. He used cue cards for his dialogue, posting them all around the set.

Bertolucci had to work around this. He and Marlon agreed, however, on the concept of the script and since the Italian director's style is improvisational, Brando made up dialogue for many of the scenes and developed his own characterization. In a few instances he carried the sex scenes even further than the director had intended.

Some have interpreted Marlon's lines in the movie as being inspired by his own experiences. At one point in the film, the Brando character says, "My father was a drunk, a screwed-up bar fighter. My mother was also a drunk. My memories as a kid are of her being arrested. We lived in a small town, a farming community. I used to have to milk a cow every morning and every night, and I liked that. But I remember one time I was all dressed up to take this girl to a basketball game. My father said, 'You have to milk the cow,' and I said, 'Would you please milk it for me?' He said, 'No, get your ass out there.' I was in a hurry, and I didn't have time to change my shoes. Later on it smelled in the car. I can't remember very many good things."

Bertolucci obviously knew how to get the best from Brando. "Instead of entering the character, I asked him to super-impose himself on it. I didn't ask him to become anything but himself. It wasn't like doing a film. It was a kind of psychoanalytical adventure."

Bertolucci also said, on another occasion, that the character of Paul was actually based on *him*. But Brando's friend, producer-actor Christian Marquand, said, "Forty years of Brando's life experiences went into the film. It is Brando talking about himself, being himself. His relations with his mother, father, children, lovers, friends—all come out in his performance as Paul."

The film premiered at the New York City Film Festival in October 1972. It was described as a tale "of the ecstasies and limitations of sexual passion," with, in the Festival version at least, sexual climaxes graphically pictured. The film drew mixed critical response and was, as one would expect from a Brando project, controversial and electric.

Tango opened to big business in Italy but ran less than a week before it was closed for censorship reasons. In Paris, it was a great hit, playing simultaneously in seven theatres.

The commercial New York engagement began on February 1, on a reserved-seat basis. The extraordinarily high price of $5 per seat didn't deter audiences and the film had a hefty advance sale of close to $75,000 even before its opening.

1973 seems a banner year for Brando. He is the star and owns a percentage of what is the year's most talked-about film. As this book goes to press, he seems assured of an Oscar nomination and further acclaim for *The Godfather*.

But he has been through all this before.

Elia Kazan has summed Marlon up for many when he said: "People were always so ready to say 'he's had it.' It makes me furious. Talent is delicate. It can hide for a while, go underground, get discouraged. It's human . . . but it doesn't go away."

Bertolucci has described Marlon as "an angel as a man and a monster as an actor. He is all instinct, but at the same time he is a complex man: one one side he needs to be loved by all; on another he is a machine incessantly producing charm; on still another he has the wisdom of an Indian sage. He is like one of those figures of the painter Francis Bacon who show on their faces all that is happening in their guts—he has the same devastated plasticity."

It's a sure thing that Marlon Brando will be around for a long time, despite his continual threats to retire. In the words of a close friend: "He cares too much about too many world problems to ease himself out of the limelight—that would weaken his ability to influence events. As long as he's an important star he wields power because he realizes that although people shouldn't be impressed by 'movie stars' they are and why not use that to do some good?"

Marlon Brando is no ordinary motion picture star. Even if *The Godfather* hadn't brought him back to eminence, his place in American film history was assured. He is to film acting almost what D. W. Griffith was to film directing. His impact has been so great that no actor of the 1950s, '60s, and '70s can escape comparison.

It's not easy for Marlon to keep on acting: "It's like sustaining a twenty-five-year love affair. There are no new tricks.

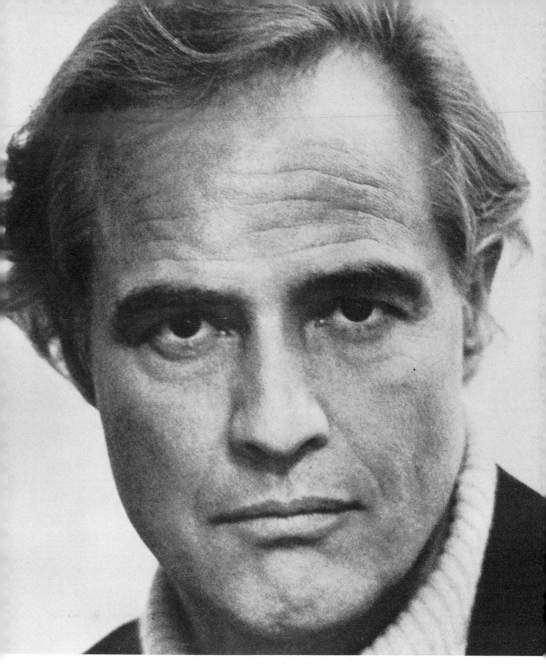
Brando today

You just have to keep finding new ways to do it, to keep it fresh."

Marlon's ambition is, in the words of a friend, "to establish a research station on his island to find ways to tap solar energy, wind energy and the nutrients in seawater." In the book *Whole Earth Catalogue* he has, according to this friend, "at last found a statement of purpose that matches his own."

In Marlon's words: ". . . the three factors that concern us all are pollution, overpopulation and aggression, and they're interlocked. If we don't solve all three problems, we can't really look to the future. Some people say it's already too late and we're just knitting and tatting and playing Monopoly to kill time before we and the planet die. But even though you're going down in a plane, and the wing is off, you pull your seat belt tight, and say: 'Maybe I'll just make it.'"

The last chapter on Brando cannot, of course, be written. There is every indication that he will continue to be an ardent spokesman against social injustices. That he will continue to be a favorite topic of conversation in movie circles. That in spite of his so-often-stated desire to leave acting he will continue to make films.

Despite his disdain for his profession when comparing it with "major issues," like civil rights, ecology, and the human condition, Brando has stated: "Human behavior has always fascinated me. Actors have to observe, and I enjoy that part of it. They have to know how much spit you've got in your mouth and where the weight of your elbows is. I could sit all day in the Optimo Cigar Store telephone booth on 42nd Street and just watch the people pass by.

"But I've always tried to run acting down, tried to be very tough about it, and I don't know why . . . It's a perfectly reasonable way to make your living. You're not stealing money and you're entertaining people. Everybody has had the experience of feeling miserable, of feeling: Christ, the world is coming to an end. And you go watch John Wayne riding across the prairie, and see the grass blowing and the clouds, and he grabs the girl and they ride off into the sunset. Yon went in there feeling awful, and you come out feeling good. *He* made you feel good. That's not bad, that's not a bad thing to do in life at all. . . ."

BRANDO

His Career to Date

PLAYS

I REMEMBER MAMA (1944)

Written by John van Druten
Adapted from Kathryn Forbes's book, *Mama's Bank Account*
Staged by John van Druten
Production designed and lighted by George Jenkins
Costumes by Lucinda Ballard
Produced by Richard Rodgers and Oscar Hammerstein II

CAST

Katrin	Joan Tetzel
Mama	Mady Christians
Papa	Richard Bishop
Dagmar	Carolyn Hummel
Christine	Frances Heflin
Mr. Hyde	Oswald Marshall
Nels	Marlon Brando
Aunt Trina	Adrienne Gessner
Aunt Sigrid	Ellen Mahar
Aunt Jenny	Ruth Gates
Uncle Chris	Oscar Homolka
A Woman	Louise Lorimer
Mr. Thorkelson	Bruno Wick
Dr. Johnson	William Pringle
Arne	Robert Antoine
A Nurse	Marie Gale
Another Nurse	Dorothy Elder
Soda Clerk	Frank Babcock
Madeline	Cora Smith
Dorothy Schiller	Ottilie Kruger
Florence Dana Moorhead	Josephine Brown
Bellboy	Herbert Kenwith

The New York Times

From Kathryn Forbes' stories about Mama's legendary bank account, but not legendary character, John van Druten has fashioned a delightful evening for the theatre. He calls it "I Remember Mama," and, like its source, it is about a Norwegian-American family living in San Francisco, one that is complete with problems, children, cats and Uncle Chris.

In the strict sense of the term, "I Remember Mama" cannot be called a play; it is rather a series of scenes about members of the same family. *(Lewis Nichols)*

New York Journal-American

The Nels of Marlon Brando is, if he doesn't mind me saying so, charming. *(Robert Garland)*

The New Yorker

[After praising Mady Christians, Oscar Homolka, and Joan Tetzel] They're very nearly perfect, but so are the nineteen other people in the cast, and in this space we won't discriminate. *(Wolcott Gibbs)*

New York newspaper PM

. . . Frances Heflin, Marlon Brando and Carolyn Hummel are all good as the children of the family . . . *(Louis Kronenberger)*

New York Daily News

. . . All in the cast are excellent . . . *(John Chapman)*

TRUCKLINE CAFE (1946)

Written by Maxwell Anderson
Settings by Boris Aronson
Directed by Harold Clurman
Presented by Mr. Clurman and Elia Kazan in association with
    the Playwrights' Company

CAST

Toby	Frank Overton
Kip	Ralph Theadore
Stew	John Sweet
Maurice	Kevin McCarthy
Min	June Walker
Wing Commander Hern	David Manners

Anne	Virginia Gilmore
Stag	Karl Malden
Angie	Irene Dailey
Celeste	Joanne Tree
Patrolman Gray	Robert Simon
Evvie Garrett	Joann Dolan
Hutch	Kenneth Tobey
Matt	Louis A. Florence
June	Jutta Wolf
Sissie	Leila Ernst
Tory McRae	Ann Shepherd
Sarge McRae	Marlon Brando
Man with a pail	Lou Gilbert
The bread man	Peter Hobbs
Janet	Peggy Meredith
Mildred	June March
Bimi	Richard Paul
Tuffy Garrett	Eugene Steiner
First man	Solen Hayes
First woman	Lorraine Kirby
Mort	Richard Waring
Second man	Joseph Adams
Second woman	Rose Steiner
First girl	Ann Morgan
Second girl	Gloria Stroock

New York Herald Tribune

Maxwell Anderson surveys the post-war world with an elegant melo-dramatic detachment in "Truckline Cafe." Through a clutter of odd characters and expository dialogue it is just possible to find a central theme in the new play at the Belasco. It has something to do with man-kind standing in desolation on the end of a bridge leading nowhere and the building up of clobbered and ignoble human relationships. There can be no question of the author's sincerity and his fervent will to have the theater play an important role in over-all reconversion. There is grave question as to the validity and power of his dramatic hodgepodge.

... Marlon Brando and Ann Shepherd bear the brunt of the melo-drama with considerable skill ... *(Howard Barnes)*

New York World-Telegram

... Except for a brief bit by Marlon Brando as the former soldier who blew his top ... the acting was indifferently bad ... *(Burton Rascoe)*

... and as the young murderer, Marlon Brando is quite effective in a difficult emotional scene ... *(Louis Kronenberger)*

New York Post

... But long after they and the play are forgotten we shall remember ... the poignant playing of Ann Shepherd and Marlon Brando as the ill-fated husband and wife.

They shall be remembered and the scenes in which they played.

Unquestionably, that is just as well. *(Vernon Rice)*

The New York Sun

... There is an effective performance from Marlon Brando as the young wife-murderer ... *(Ward Morehouse)*

New York Journal-American

... After playing Frankie to Ann Shepherd's Johnnie, Marlon Brando has himself a high old actorial time before giving himself up to Robert Simon pretending to be a California cop. A graduate of the role of Nels in "I Remember Mama," young Mr. Brando distinguishes himself in this, his second professional part ... *(Robert Garland)*

CANDIDA (1946)

Written by Bernard Shaw
Staged by Guthrie McClintic
Revived by Katharine Cornell, in association with Gilbert Miller

CAST

Miss Proserpine Garnett	Mildred Natwick
James Mavor Morell	Wesley Addy
Alexander Mill	Oliver Cliff
Mr. Burgess	Cedric Hardwicke
Candida	Katharine Cornell
Eugene Marchbanks	Marlon Brando

New York World-Telegram

Nobody can ever do Marchbanks properly. He is an impossible character for any actor to play. Shaw says nobody has ever done the part to his satisfaction. How could anyone? Marchbanks is Shaw's own conception of himself. Shaw's idea is that he is a combination of Percy Bysshe Shelley, Karl Marx, Frederick Nietzsche, Samuel Butler, E. H. Sothern, John Donne, Henrik Ibsen and Oscar Wilde . . .

Maybe Miss Cornell should put on pants and play Marchbanks, even if she has to wear whiskers. Mr. Brando did as well as he could as Marchbanks . . . *(Burton Rascoe)*

New York Journal-American

. . . Up to then, I had thought that the Eugene Marchbanks of Mr. Meredith was the Eugene Marchbanks for whom his creator had been waiting. As a matter of fact, I remember saying so in print. But, in the late April of 1942, I had not sat in the presence of the Eugene Marchbanks of the Marlon Brando who played it yesterday. Young Mr. Brando stepped right out of the stage directions.

. . . But the fresh excitement of the current reproduction stems straight from the Eugene Marchbanks of Marlon Brando, he of Nels Forbes in "I Remember Mama," of Sage McRae in—if I may mention it—"Truckline Cafe." Young Mr. Brando's young Mr. Marchbanks is superb. It is he and his performance that the enthusiasts at the Cort may still be cheering for all I know to the contrary. *(Robert Garland)*

New York Post

Probably one of the hardest parts ever written for a man to play is Marchbanks. Shaw describes him as "A strange shy youth of 18, slight, effeminate, with a delicate childish voice, and a hunted, tormented expression and shrinking manner . . . *(sic)*"

Shaw practically defies an actor to play Marchbanks without causing a wave of nausea to pass through any audience. That no such thing happened yesterday afternoon is certainly to Marlon Brando's credit, and he continues to be the promising young actor he was in his two previous plays. *(Vernon Rice)*

New York Daily News

. . . and a new young actor named Marlon Brando managed to make something different, something a little more understandable, out of the trying role of Marchbanks, the baby poet.

Mr. Brando's performance . . . lent to yesterday's revival of the play a very pleasant air . . .

The role of Marchbanks, in the words of the poet himself, can be "horror, horror, horror." It can be too effeminate. It can be shouted—and some of Shaw's lines in this 1903-vintage comedy should not be spoken too loudly, lest they show their age. Mr. Brando achieved a believable lovesick introvert by playing very quietly. I felt that his intensity was within him, where it should be, and not spread all around outside. For the second time this season—the first was in "Truckline

Cafe"—the young man has shown himself a player of promise. *(John Chapman)*

The New York Times

. . . Marlon Brando emphasizes the weakness and banks the fire, the result being a somewhat monotonously intoning poet. His version is not believable . . . *(Lewis Nichols)*

A FLAG IS BORN (1946)

Written by Ben Hecht
Music by Kurt Weill
Scenery by Robert Davison
Costumes by John Boyt
Choreography by Zamira Gon
Musical direction by Isaac Van Grove
Staged by Luther Adler
Produced by Jules J. Leventhal
Sponsored by the American League for a Free Palestine

CAST

Speaker	Quentin Reynolds
Tevya	Paul Muni
Zelda	Celia Adler
David	Marlon Brando
The Singer	Mario Berini
Saul	George David Baxter
Old One	Morris Samuylow
Middle-Aged One	David Manning
Young One	John Baragrey
David the King	William Allyn
Solomon	Gregory Morton
American Statesman	Jonathan Harris
Russian Statesman	Yasha Rosenthal
First English Statesman	Emlyn Williams
Second English Statesman	Jefferson Coates
French Statesman	Frederick Rudin
First Soldier	Steve Hill
Second Soldier	Jonathan Harris
Third Soldier	Harold Gray

The New York Times

To aid the American League for a Free Palestine, Paul Muni is appearing in Ben Hecht's pageant, "A Flag Is Born," which had its second public showing at the Alvin last evening. Since the post-war fate of the Jews is only a little less harrowing than it was during the decade before the war, and since Mr. Muni's performance is acting of obvious eminence, the mixed values of Mr. Hecht's script leave this reviewer ungratefully reluctant. The cause of the Jews and the good-will of the people who have labored to mount this pageant deserve a finer script than Mr. Hecht has delivered. *(Brooks Atkinson)*

New York Herald Tribune

. . . Marlon Brando is an embittered youngster who meets the elders in a Jewish graveyard . . . *(Howard Barnes)*

The New Yorker

. . . Paul Muni, Celia Adler, and Marlon Brando obviously feel deeply the gravity of their message and their performances as the tortured trio in the graveyard are dignified and impressive. . . . It seems a pity that their efforts are so largely wasted. *(Wolcott Gibbs)*

Newsweek

. . . is worth seeing for the fine and elegant performances of Paul Muni, Celia Adler, Marlon Brando, and many others . . .

New York Daily News

. . . Marlon Brando portrays the young man and he, too, has bitter things to say . . . *(John Chapman)*

PM

. . . The cast, which includes Marlon Brando . . . performs agreeably . . . *(Louis Kronenberger)*

The New York Sun

. . . Marlon Brando, the young actor who was so generally acclaimed last season, is a bitter and impassioned David . . . *(Ward Morehouse)*

New York World-Telegram

. . . Marlon Brando is a sternly, hopeless David whose accusations sear when his bitterness bursts out . . . *(William Hawkins)*

New York Post

. . . they meet up with a bitterly cynical young Jewish lad, David, played by Marlon Brando . . .
. . . Marlon Brando was called upon again to provide some dramatic fireworks . . . *(Vernon Rice)*

New York Journal-American

. . . In the presence of this gentleman of the press to whom all the world is supposed to be a stage and all the people merely players, the recurrent young actor whose name is Marlon Brando is the bright particular star of the Ben Hecht pageant. First in "Truckline Cafe," then in "Candida," now in "A Flag Is Born," he is rapidly fulfilling the brilliant promise he made as the short-trousered Nels in the long lasting "I Remember Mama." His David is enduring in the memory. *(Robert Garland)*

A STREETCAR NAMED DESIRE (1947)

Written by Tennessee Williams
Setting by Jo Mielziner
Costumes by Lucinda Ballard
Staged by Elia Kazan
Produced by Irene M. Selznick

CAST

Negro woman	Gee Gee Jama
Eunice Hubbel	Peg Hillias
Stanley Kowalski	Marlon Brando
Stella Kowalski	Kim Hunter
Harold Mitchell	Karl Malden
Steve Hubbel	Rudy Bond
Blanche Du Bois	Jessica Tandy
Pablo Gonzales	Nick Dennis
A young collector	Vito Christi
Mexican woman	Edna Thomas
A strange woman	Ann Dere
A strange man	Richard Garrick

The New York Times

Tennessee Williams has brought us a superb drama, "A Streetcar Named Desire," which was acted at the Ethel Barrymore last evening. And Jessica Tandy gives a superb performance as rueful heroine whose misery Mr. Williams is tenderly recording. This must be one of the most perfect marriages of acting and playwrighting. For the acting and playwrighting are perfectly blended in a limpid performance, and it is impossible to tell where Miss Tandy begins to give form and warmth to the mood Mr. Williams has created. . . .

The rest of the acting is also of very high quality indeed. Marlon Brando as the quick-tempered, scornful, violent mechanic; Karl Malden as a stupid but wondering suitor; Kim Hunter as the patient though troubled sister—all act not only with color and style but with insight. *(Brooks Atkinson)*

New York Herald Tribune

. . . Miss Tandy is always equal to an enormously taxing role in the part of Blanche . . .

. . . She had admirable assistance. Marlon Brando is brutally convincing as the brother-in-law, who forces her on the night his wife is having a child . . . *(Howard Barnes)*

Newsweek

. . . But next to Miss Tandy, the surest performance is that of Marlon Brando, the realistic mug who knows what Blanche is and where she belongs . . .

The New Yorker

. . . Marlon Brando, as Kowalski, is, as hinted previously, almost pure ape . . . and though he undoubtedly emphasizes the horrors of the Vieux Carré as opposed to Belle Reve, it is a brutally effective characterization. *(Wolcott Gibbs)*

New York World-Telegram

. . . Marlon Brando plays the blunt and passionate Stanley Kowalski with an astonishing authenticity. His stilted speech and swift rages are ingeniously spontaneous, while his deep-rooted simplicity is sustained every second. *(William Hawkins)*

PM

. . . No one is likely to underrate Marlon Brando's brilliant performance of the brother-in-law, the more astonishing for being like nothing else he has ever played. *(Louis Kronenberger)*

The New York Sun

Marlon Brando turns in his finest work to date in his characterization of the slow-witted virile, uncomprehending young husband. *(Ward Morehouse)*

New York Post

I have hitherto not shared the enthusiasm of most reviewers for Marlon Brando, but his portrayal of the heroine's sullen, violent nemesis is an excellent piece of work . . . *(Richard Watts, Jr.)*

New York Daily News

. . . The Company, headed by Jessica Tandy, Marlon Brando, Kim Hunter and Karl Malden is the answer to a playgoer's dream.

. . . Mr. Brando is magnificent as the forthright husband, in his simple rages, his simple affections and his blunt humor . . . *(John Chapman)*

New York Journal-American

. . . On the other hand, no fault is to be found with the Stanley Kowalski of Marlon Brando. Here, in "A Streetcar Named Desire," is our theatre's most memorable young actor at his most memorable . . . *(Robert Garland)*

FILMS

THE MEN

A United Artists Release (1950)
Directed by Fred Zinnemann
Produced by Stanley Kramer
Story and screenplay by Carl Foreman
Running time: 85 minutes

CAST

Ken	Marlon Brando
Ellen	Teresa Wright
Dr. Brock	Everett Sloan
Norm	Jack Webb
Leo	Richard Erdman
Angel	Arthur Jurado
Nurse Robbins	Virginia Farmer
Ellen's Mother	Dorothy Tree
Ellen's Father	Howard St. John
Dolores	Nita Hunter
Laverne	Patricia Joiner
Mr. Doolin	John Miller
Dr. Kameran	Cliff Clark
Man at Bar	Ray Teal
Angel's Mother	Marguerite Martin

The New York Times

. . . a trenchant and stinging performance as one of these disabled men who struggles against his bleak frustrations toward a calm readjustment to life is given in it by Marlon Brando, making his screen debut. . . . *(Bosley Crowther)*

Solo shot Brando, *The Men*

Training for *The Men*

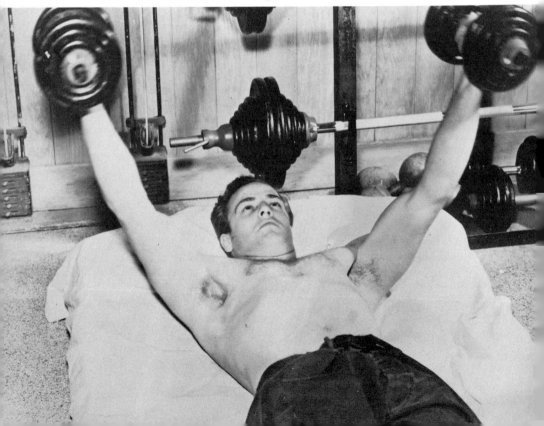

New York Herald Tribune

Brando, in an acting contrast which makes Miss Wright look even paler, lives up to all expectations as the ex-lieutenant gradually and painfully bringing himself back from despair. His irritability and emotional wavering seem the real outward manifestations of an inward struggle, whereas Miss Wright's do not. His progress from a drugged, bedridden state through gymnastics and other treatment to the point at which he can take his place in the world, symbolized by driving a car and changing a tire by himself, is a re-enactment which has the audience straining with him all the way. Every line he speaks carries meaning in the way he speaks it, in a performance which depends not at all on personality but entirely on understanding of character and technical virtuosity. *(Otis L. Guernsey, Jr.)*

Newsweek

Zinnemann cleverly surmounts the difficult chore of integrating the film's personal elements and its complicated therapy, and he makes effective use of the paraplegic's tough, healthy sense of humor. Brando . . . a strong performance but one that fails to give the story an emotional warmth it could well use in the clinches. . . .

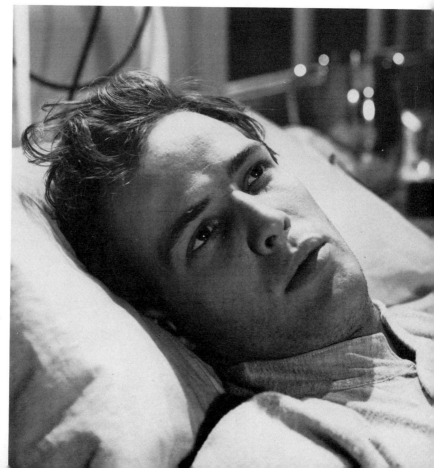

Solo shot Brando,
The Men

A STREETCAR NAMED DESIRE

A Warner Brothers Release (1951)
Directed by Elia Kazan
Produced by Charles K. Feldman
Screenplay by Tennessee Williams
Adapted by Oscar Saul from the play by Mr. Williams
Running time: 2 hours, 5 minutes

CAST

Blanche Du Bois	Vivien Leigh
Stanley Kowalski	Marlon Brando
Stella Kowalski	Kim Hunter
Mitch	Karl Malden
Steve	Rudy Bond
Pablo	Nick Dennis
Eunice	Peg Hillias
A Collector	Wright King
A Doctor	Richard Garrick
The Matron	Ann Dere
The Mexican woman	Edna Thomas

The New York Times

. . . Director Elia Kazan and a simply superlative cast have fashioned a motion picture that throbs with passion and poignancy. Indeed, through the haunting performance England's great Vivien Leigh gives in the heart-breaking role of Mr. Williams' deteriorating Southern belle and through the mesmerizing moods Mr. Kazan has wreathed with the techniques of the screen, this picture . . . becomes as fine, if not finer, than the play. Inner torments are seldom projected with such sensitivity and clarity on the screen.

Of course, the first factor in this triumph is Mr. Williams' play, which embraces, among its many virtues, an essential human conflict in visual terms. The last brave, defiant, hopeless struggle of the lonely and decaying Blanche du Bois to hold on to her faded gentility against the heartless badgering of her rough-neck brother-in-law is a tangible cat-and-dog set-to, marked with manifold physical episodes as well as a wealth of fluctuations of verbally fashioned images and moods. . . .

. . . No less brilliant, however [than Vivien Leigh], within his area is Marlon Brando in the role of the loud, lusty, brawling, brutal, amoral Polish brother-in-law. Mr. Brando created the role in the stage play

With Kim Hunter, *A Streetcar Named Desire*

and he carries over all the energy and the steel-spring characteristics that made him vivid on the stage. But here, where we're so much closer to him, he seems that much more highly charged, his despairs seem that much more pathetic and his comic moments that much more slyly enjoyed. *(Bosley Crowther)*

New York Herald Tribune

. . . Brando gives a remarkably truthful performance of a heavy-muscled, practical animal, secure in the normalcy of marriage and friendship, proud but indelicate, cunning but insensitive, aware of Blanche's deceits but not of her suffering. This performance is as close to perfect as one could wish . . . *(Otis L. Guernsey, Jr.)*

With Vivien Leigh, *A Streetcar Named Desire*

Time

... Though the movie has its flaws, it can claim a merit rare in Hollywood films: it is a grown-up, gloves-off drama of real human beings.

... As the hulking, animalistic Kowalski, Marlon Brando fills his scenes with a virile power that gives "Streetcar" its highest voltage.

VIVA ZAPATA!

A 20th Century-Fox Release (1952)
Directed by Elia Kazan
Produced by Darryl F. Zanuck
Written by John Steinbeck
Based on the novel by Edgcumb Pinchon
Running time: 1 hour, 52 minutes

CAST

Zapata	Marlon Brando
Josefa	Jean Peters
Bufemio	Anthony Quinn
Fernando	Joseph Wiseman
Don Nacio	Arnold Moss
Pancho Villa	Alan Reed
Soldadera	Margo
Madero	Harold Gordon
Pablo	Lou Gilbert
Senora Espejo	Mildred Dunnock
Huerta	Frank Silvera
Aunt	Nina Varcia
Senor Espejo	Florenz Ames
Zapatista	Bernie Gozier
Col. Guajardo	Frank De Kova
Old General	Richard Garrick
Diaz	Fay Roope

The New York Times

Mr. Kazan is eloquent with a camera. . . .

. . . His [Brando's] acting of a baffled, tongue-tied Indian [in love scenes] does not carry too much force.

But when this dynamic young performer is speaking his anger or his love for a fellow revolutionary, or when he is charging through the land at the head of his rebel-soldiers or walking bravely into the trap of his doom, there is power enough in his portrayal to cause the screen to throb. And throb it does, in particular, in the last tragic, heart-breaking scene, when the rebel leader is shot down, the victim of his own unfailing trust. *(Bosley Crowther)*

New York Herald Tribune

. . . Directed by Elia Kazan in strong moods of blood and fire, and acted by Marlon Brando in a smoldering, saturnine portrayal of a man of violence, "Viva Zapata" studies the tricky relationship between the "man on the horse" and the people who provide him with inspiration and enfranchise his acts. . . .

Zapata is presented as a hero in the sense that he possesses all the animal virtues and uses his strength only against injustice or treachery. But he is not polished out of all recognition as a human being: Brando gives his character all the rough edges and soiled spots of a half-civilized man whose spoken words are deceptively simple and whose demeanor is deceptively calm. In this, as well as in other respects, "Viva Zapata" binds good and bad together in a Chinese puzzle of harsh experience. . . . *(Otis L. Guernsey, Jr.)*

With Margo, Joseph Wiseman, *Viva Zapata!*

With extras, *Viva Zapata!*

Newsweek

. . . a careful and intelligent characterization of the humanitarian who was wise enough to know that no nation could survive in the shadow of a single leader. . . .

Time

"Viva Zapata" is a delayed cinematic footnote to M-G-M's slambang "Viva Villa" . . . The picture shows Zapata (Marlon Brando) as a somewhat crude but noble fellow with a nice regard for the social amenities. He is also characterized as a thinker, talker as well as a brawler. . . .

JULIUS CAESAR

A Metro-Goldwyn-Mayer Release (1953)
Directed by Joseph L. Mankiewicz
Produced by John Houseman
Play by William Shakespeare
Running time: 2 hours, 1 minute

CAST

Julius Caesar	Louis Calhern
Mark Antony	Marlon Brando
Brutus	James Mason
Cassius	John Gielgud
Casca	Edmond O'Brien
Calpurnia	Greer Garson
Portia	Deborah Kerr
Marullus	George MacReady
Flavius	Michael Pate
A Soothsayer	Richard Hale
Cicero	Alan Napier
Decius Brutus	John Hoyt
Metellus Cimber	Tom Powers
Cinna	William Cottrell
Trebonius	Jack Raine
Ligarius	Ian Wolfe
Artimidorus	Morgan Farley
Servant to Antony	Bill Phipps

The New York Times

... the delight and surprise of the film is Mr. Brando's Mark Antony, which is something memorable to see. Athletic and bullet-headed, he looks the realest Roman of them all and possesses the fire of hot convictions and the firm elasticity of steel. Happily Mr. Brando's diction, which has been guttural and slurred in previous films, is clear and precise in this instance. In him a major talent has emerged. *(Bosley Crowther)*

New York Herald Tribune

... Marlon Brando's Antony is constrained and studied in its details, but it has an animal vigor that bursts forth when needed in the high points of the funeral oration and in the domination of Octavius as they plan the reorganization of political Rome. *(Otis L. Guernsey, Jr.)*

With Louis Calhern, Greer Garson, *Julius Caesar*

The "Friends, Romans, countrymen" speech. *Julius Caesar*

Newsweek

. . . Marlon Brando, the question of whose diction worried many advance speculators about the picture, plays Mark Antony with cold fire and pungent, if not classically Shakespearean, speech. . . .

THE WILD ONE

A Columbia Pictures Release (1953)
Directed by Laslo Benedek
Produced by Stanley Kramer
Screenplay by John Paxton
Based on a story by Frank Rooney
Running time: 1 hour, 19 minutes

CAST

Johnny	Marlon Brando
Kathie	Mary Murphy
Harry Bleeker	Robert Keith
Chino	Lee Marvin
Sheriff Singer	Jay C. Flippen
Mildred	Peggy Maley
Charlie Thomas	Hugh Sanders
Frank Bleeker	Ray Teal
Bill Hannegan	John Brown
Art Kleiner	Will Wright
Ben	Robert Osterich
Wilson	Robert Bice
Jimmy	William Vedder
Britches	Yvonne Doughty

The New York Times

A little bit of the surface of contemporary American life is scratched in Stanley Kramer's "The Wild One." . . . Although the reality of it goes soft and then collapses at the end, it is a tough and engrossing motion picture. . . .

. . . Mr. Brando is vicious and relentless so long as he is permitted to be. . . .

. . . But unfortunately the picture is not permitted to remain in these realms. . . .

Withal, "The Wild One" is a picture of extraordinary candor and courage—a picture that tries to grasp an idea, even though its reach falls short. . . . *(Bosley Crowther)*

New York Herald Tribune

"The Wild One" is a strange tense little film . . . fronted with force.

With extras, *The Wild One*

With Mary Murphy, *The Wild One*

In *The Wild One*

With Jay C. Flippen, Mary Murphy, extras, *The Wild One*

... The central figure of this brief episode—it takes place within twenty-four hours—is an ominous youth named Johnny, played carefully and forcefully by Marlon Brando. ... *(P.V.B.)*

Newsweek

... Playing a role that is twice as tough and taciturn as his Kowalski in "A Streetcar Named Desire," Brando gets to smile at the film's end and to show a touch of normal human emotion. Otherwise his performance is unrelated to anything except an enigmatic exercise in the sinister. ...

Saturday Review

... "The Wild One" ... has a startling freshness about it. ... The nice thing about Mr. Kramer's movie is that it doesn't preach or ever state directly what the sources of the trouble are. It's done largely through implication and is helped no end by an astonishing performance on the part of Marlon Brando.

... It's first-rate moviemaking and I'd say also something in the way of a public service. It's pleasant to be able to report such conscientiousness in a Hollywood seemingly so consecrated at present to tricks and novelties. *(Hollis Alpert)*

ON THE WATERFRONT

A Columbia Pictures Release; a Horizon Production (1954)
Directed by Elia Kazan
Produced by Sam Spiegel
Screenplay by Budd Schulberg
Based on an original story by Mr. Schulberg and suggested by the
series of Pulitzer Prize-winning articles by Malcolm Johnson
Running time: 1 hour, 48 minutes

CAST

Terry Malloy	Marlon Brando
Edie Doyle	Eva Marie Saint
Father Barry	Karl Malden
Johnny Friendly	Lee J. Cobb
Charley Malloy	Rod Steiger
"Pop" Doyle	John Hamilton
"Kayo" Dugan	Pat Henning
Glover	Leif Erickson
Big Mac	James Westerfield
Truck	Tony Galento
Tillio	Tami Mauriello
Barney	Abe Simon
Mott	John Heidabrand
Moose	Rudy Bond
Luke	Don Blackman
Jimmy	Arthur Keegan
J. P.	Barry Macollum
Specs	Mike O'Dowd
Gilette	Marty Balsam
Slim	Fred Gwynne
Tommy	Thomas Handley
Mrs. Collins	Anne Hegira

The New York Times

. . . Marlon Brando's Terry Malloy is a shatteringly poignant portrait of an amoral, confused, illiterate citizen of the lower depths who is goaded into decency by love, hate and murder. His groping for words, use of the vernacular, care of his beloved pigeons, pugilist's walk and gestures and his discoveries of love and the immensity of the crimes surrounding him are highlights of a beautiful and moving portrayal.

With Eva Marie Saint, *On the Waterfront*

Time

. . . Kazan succeeds in producing a shrewd piece of screen journalism, a melodrama in the grand manner of "Public Enemy" and "Little Caesar." . . .

Brando in this show is one glorious meathead . . . The audience may never forget that Brando is acting, but it will know that he is doing a powerful acting job.

Newsweek

The star of "On the Waterfront," however, is Marlon Brando and it is difficult to imagine a role—except possibly that of Kowalski in "A Streetcar Named Desire"—that is better suited to his particular talents. . . .

Let me say right off that "On the Waterfront" is one of the most exciting films ever made in the United States. . . .

. . . And if "On the Waterfront" were not an event for this reason, it would be one because of the performance of Marlon Brando, one of the finest things any man has done on the screen.

. . . Brando's performance in this role is a piece of genuine artistry. With half-sentences finished by body shrugs and fish gestures of the hands, with a drawn-brow groping for words, with a street arab's laugh or quick insult, with an ex-athlete's bounce to his walk, Brando projects a wonderfully absorbing portrait of a semi-stupid, stubborn, inner-sweet young man.

With Eva Marie Saint, *On the Waterfront*

With Lee J. Cobb, *On the Waterfront*

... "On the Waterfront" will undoubtedly create a storm of excitement because of its use of the screen and because of Brando's vitalizing performance. I suspect that among the viewers there will be many who will find the ending somewhat pat and preachy and the plotting a bit slick ... But despite "Waterfront's" shortcomings, there is no doubt that a landmark in American movie-making has been established by this documentary of the docks. *(Lee Rogow)*

New York Herald Tribune

... He uses his voice like a fist and concentrates aggression into every movement. ... This role bursts out of Brando with instinctive energy and startling accuracy, in a performance which is a show in itself. *(Otis L. Guernsey, Jr.)*

DESIRÉE

A 20th Century-Fox Release (1954)
Directed by Henry Koster
Produced by Julian Blaustein
Screenplay by Daniel Taradash
Based on the novel by Annemarie Selinko
Running time: 1 hour, 50 minutes

CAST

Napoleon	Marlon Brando
Desirée	Jean Simmons
Josephine	Merle Oberon
Bernadotte	Michael Rennie
Joseph Bonaparte	Cameron Mitchell
Julie	Elizabeth Sellars
Paulette	Charlotte Austin
Mme. Bonaparte	Cathleen Nesbitt
Marie	Evelyn Varden
Mme. Clary	Isobel Elsom
Talleyrand	John Hoyt
Despreaux	Alan Napier
Oscar	Nicholas Koster
Etienne	Richard Deacon
Queen Hedwig	Edith Evanson
Mme. Tallien	Carolyn Jones
Pouche	Sam Gilman
Louis Bonaparte	Larry Craine
Caroline Bonaparte	Judy Lester
Lucien Bonaparte	Richard Van Cleemput
Elisa Bonaparte	Florence Dublin

New York Herald Tribune

Napoleon's invasion of CinemaScope echoes with the sound of trumpets and the heavy tread of glamourized history. The Emperor of the French in "Desiree" at the Roxy—forcefully acted by Marlon Brando with a cleft in his chin and one hand in his tunic—is viewed with awe in an eye-filling panorama of scenery, costumes and beribboned actors. . . .

As for the acting, Marlon Brando works the extremely difficult trick of using Napoleon's celebrated eccentricities as part of an impetuous spirit, without appearing ridiculous. He animates his whole perfor-

With Ethiopia's Emperor Haile Selassie on the set of *Desirée*

mance with an electric current of megalomania, which shocks the other characters when they make contact with him.

. . . It has a surface splendor and some flashes from the eagle brow of Marlon Brando and that is all. *(Otis L. Guernsey, Jr.)*

The New York Times

A great deal of handsome decoration and two talented and attractive stars have been put into the CinemaScope production of the historical romance "Desiree." The only essential missing is a story of any consequence.

... Marlon Brando's Napoleon is just a fancy (and sometimes fatuous) facade. *(Bosley Crowther)*

Newsweek

Marlon Brando's Napoleon is not likely to be remembered with his passionate Polish mechanic of "A Streetcar Named Desire," nor yet with his troubled ex-boxer and dockhand of "On the Waterfront." For one thing, as the publicity men keep saying, he looks more like Napoleon than Napoleon himself, with a result that sometimes borders on burlesque....

... In a last burst of Napoleonic aplomb, he asks her not to hold the weapon like an umbrella. With this surrender, Marlon Brando also relinquishes one of his most resplendent if least rewarding roles.

With Jean Simmons and Merle Oberon, *Desirée*

GUYS AND DOLLS

A Metro-Goldwyn-Mayer Release (1955)
Directed by Joseph L. Mankiewicz
Produced by Samuel Goldwyn
Screenplay by Mr. Mankiewicz
Based on the play of the same name with book by
    Jo Swerling and Abe Burrows
Running time: 2 hours, 30 minutes

CAST

Sky Masterson	Marlon Brando
Sarah Brown	Jean Simmons
Nathan Detroit	Frank Sinatra
Miss Adelaide	Vivian Blaine
Lieutenant Brannigan	Robert Keith
Nicely-Nicely Johnson	Stubby Kaye
Big Jule	S. S. Pully
Benny Southstreet	Johnny Silver
Harry The Horse	Sheldon Leonard
Rusty Charlie	Dan Dayton
Society Max	George E. Stone
Arvid Abernathy	Regis Toomey
General Cartwright	Kathryn Givney
Laverne	Veda Ann Borg
Agatha	Mary Alan Hokanson
Angie The Ox	Joe McTurk
Calvin	Kay Kuter
Mission Member	Stapicton Kent
Cuban Singer	Renee Renor

And The Goldwyn Girls

The New York Times

As Sky Masterson, the big-time gambler, Marlon Brando is some-what genteel. . . . *(Bosley Crowther)*

New York Herald Tribune

The big news about "Guys and Dolls," as every movie fan must know by now, is this: Brando sings! . . .

Brando and Sinatra look too young for their roles as veteran gam-

With Frank Sinatra, Vivian Blaine, Jean Simmons, Regis Toomey, *Guys and Dolls*

blers. They bring a boyish quality into the man's world of big money, and this is the only detail in which the movie is somewhat out of key. . . . *(William K. Zinsser)*

Newsweek

People will probably go to this . . . movie . . . simply to watch Marlon Brando dance and to hear him sing. They will learn that at times he has a provocative husk on his voice; as a dancer he executes only a few simple ballroom steps. . . . As singers, neither Brando nor Miss Simmons can hold a candle, let alone a torch, to Vivian Blaine, who sings her old Broadway part. . . .

TEAHOUSE OF THE AUGUST MOON

A Metro-Goldwyn-Mayer Release (1956)
Directed by Daniel Mann
Produced by Jack Cummings
Screenplay by John Patrick
Based on the stage play by Patrick and the book by Vern J. Sneider
Running time: 2 hours, 3 minutes

CAST

Sakini	Marlon Brando
Capt. Fisby	Glenn Ford
Lotus Blossom	Machiko Kyo
Capt. McLean	Eddie Albert
Col. Purdy	Paul Ford
Mr. Seiko	June Negami
Miss Higa Jiga	Nijiko Kiyokawa
Little Japanese girl	Mitsuko Sawamura
Sgt. Gregovich	Henry (Harry) Morgan
Mr. Sumata	Minoru Nishida
Mr. Hokaida	Kichizaemon Sarumarn
Mr. Omura	Frank Tokunaga
Mr. Oshira	Raynum K. Tsukamoto

New York Post

Brando's makeup is amazing, his voice manipulation is the work of a skilled artist. His manner, for this reviewer, who has witnessed the mischief of two other Sakinis, is certainly as praiseworthy. Glenn Ford, incidentally, never has given a more engaging account of himself than herein. *(Irene Thirer)*

New York Daily News ★ ★ ★ ★

That sly, philosophical Oriental, Sakini, ingratiatingly played by Brando on the screen, is important to the furtherance of the plot and to the atmosphere of lunatic comedy that keeps the audience in a state of chuckles all through the film. He is the instrument through which the occupying forces of the U.S. Army were taken over by the simple peasantry of the island instead of the Army, as intended, making the natives over into the image of good democratic citizens of a benevolent, protective military government.

The comedy situations are spiced with irony, which is part of the

With Glenn Ford, *Teahouse of the August Moon*

With Paul Ford and Glenn Ford, *Teahouse of the August Moon*

film's beguiling quality. As is usual with comedies about the military, the higher the officer, the more ridiculous he is made to appear. The cast responds expertly to director Daniel Mann's sure but light touch, under which Glenn Ford gives an amusing characterization of Capt. Fisby, matching Brando's clever interpretation of Sakini. *(Kate Cameron)*

The New York Times

As for Mr. Brando's appearance as Sakini, the amiable Okinawan who engineers the confusion and subversion of the American Army's aims, it is also broad and bounding, shot through with grimaces and japes, but somehow it lacks the warmth and candor that are called for in the role.

In the first place, Mr. Brando looks synthetic. A conspicuous make-up of his eyes and a shiny black wig do not imbue him with an oriental cast. And his manner of speaking broken English, as though he had a wad of chewing gum clenched between his teeth, is not only disconcerting but also makes him hard to understand.

More than this, Mr. Brando is too elaborate, too consciously cute. His Sakini is less a charming rascal than a calculated clown. *(Bosley Crowther)*

SAYONARA

A Warner Brothers Release (1957)
Directed by Joshua Logan
Produced by William Goetz
Screenplay by Paul Osborn
Running time: 2 hours, 27 minutes

CAST

Major Gruver	Marlon Brando
Hana-Ogi	Miiko Taka
Kelly	Red Buttons
Katsumi	Miyoshi Umeki
Eileen Webster	Patricia Owens
General Webster	Kent Smith
Mrs. Webster	Martha Scott
Bailey	James Garner
Nakamura	Ricardo Montalban
Colonel Craford	Douglas Watson
Fumiko-san	Reiko Kuba
Teruko-san	Soo Yong

The New York Times

It is Mr. Brando's Major Gruver, the Air Force hero who falls in love with a beautiful Japanese actress in this beautiful, sentimental tale, that gives eccentricity and excitement to a richly colorful film. It is Mr. Brando's acting of what could be a conventional role that spins what could be a routine romance into a lively and tense dramatic show. *(Bosley Crowther)*

New York Herald Tribune

Marlon Brando's performance in "Sayonara" is so inventive, so full of sly surprises and little shafts of humor, that this rambling movie holds its spell almost to the end. . . . He plays a jet ace who is sent from Korea to Japan for a rest . . . his acting is always on the side of restraint—his voice at times almost inaudible, his Southern accent only thick enough to suggest his origins but never a caricature. His basic tuition, his uncanny sense of timing and comedy, his deep kindness— these qualities carry a story which, without him, would seem turgid and contrived. *(William K. Zinsser)*

With Red Buttons, Miyoshi Umeki, *Sayonara*

Newsweek

"Sayonara" is . . . about the social tragedies that have arisen when East (occupied Japan, in this instance) meets West (U.S. service-men). . . .

. . . Brando and his girl . . . spend most of two and one-half hours frozen in a dreadful standstill, debating whether to marry . . . Dull tale of the meeting of the twain.

With Red Buttons, Miyoshi Umeki, *Sayonara*

THE YOUNG LIONS

A 20th Century-Fox Release (1958)
Directed by Edward Dmytryk
Produced by Al Lichtman
Screenplay by Edward Anhalt
Based on the novel by Irwin Shaw
Running time: 2 hours, 47 minutes

CAST

Christian	Marlon Brando
Noah	Montgomery Clift
Michael Whiteacre	Dean Martin
Hope Plowman	Hope Lange
Margaret Freemantle	Barbara Rush
Gretchen Hardenberg	May Britt
Hardenberg	Maximilian Schell
Simone	Dora Doll
Sergeant Rickett	Lee Van Cleef
Francoise	Liliane Montevecchi
Brant	Parley Baer
Lieutenant Green	Arthur Franz
Private Burnecker	Hal Baylor
Private Cowley	Richard Gardner
Captain Colclough	Herbert Rudley
Corporal Kraus	John Alderson
Private Faber	Sam Gilman
Private Donnelly	L. O. Jones
Private Brailsford	Julien Burton

New York Herald Tribune

. . . Although he [Brando] has been given a sleek and personable role rather than a strong one, the emphasis on charm will give his admirers a great many chances to watch him roll his eyes and pronounce English with a nice German accent. *(Paul V. Beckley)*

Variety

. . . Brando plays his role with studied deliberation and considerable conviction. . . . *('Abel')*

In *The Young Lions*

In *The Young Lions*

Time

. . . Two performances—by Marlon Brando and Montgomery Clift—
of unusually deep draft . . . Brando . . . underplays to the point where
in many a scene only a telepathist could hope to tell what he is thinking; but in the long run he imparts . . . an urgent and moving sense
that there is a soul somewhere inside the lieutenant's uniform.

The New York Times

. . . As played by Marlon Brando with his hair dyed a shiny corn-silk
blond and his voice affecting a German accent reminiscent of Weber
and Fields, this fellow is sensitive and attractive. He evokes complete
sympathy. He has the gentleness of one of those nice young Germans
in the memorable "All Quiet on the Western Front."
. . . Mr. Brando makes the German much more vital and interesting
than Montgomery Clift and Dean Martin make the Americans. . . .
(*Bosley Crowther*)

THE FUGITIVE KIND

A United Artists Release (1960)
Directed by Sidney Lumet
Produced by Martin Jurow and Richard A. Shepherd
Screenplay by Tennessee Williams and Meade Roberts
Based on the play by Mr. Williams
Running time: 1 hour, 59 minutes

CAST

Val Xavier	Marlon Brando
Lady Torrance	Anna Magnani
Carol Cutrere	Joanne Woodward
Vee Talbott	Maureen Stapleton
Jabe Torrance	Victor Jory
Sheriff Talbott	R. G. Armstrong
Uncle Pleasant	Emory Richardson
Ruby Lightfoot	Spivy
Dolly Hamma	Sally Gracie
Beulah Binnings	Lucille Benson
David Cutrere	John Baragrey
Dog Hamma	Ben Yaffe
Pee Wee Binnings	Joe Brown Jr.

The New York Times

A lot of Tennessee Williams' sordid view of life may be observed in the film made from his "Orpheus Descending," now called "The Fugitive Kind."

. . . because Marlon Brando and Anna Magnani play these two people brilliantly, "The Fugitive Kind" has a distinction and a sensitivity that are rare today in films. *(Bosley Crowther)*

New York Herald Tribune

. . . The acting is impressive. I should imagine actors live for such roles. Not one of them fails to deliver. . . .

Brando appears in a drenching rain, wiping his guitar with his snakeskin jacket before seeking shelter. . . . He only wants "just a li'l, you know, dry place," he explains in that inarticulate half ominous, half dreamy manner at which Brando excels. . . . *(Paul V. Beckley)*

In *The Fugitive Kind*

With Anna Magnani, *The Fugitive Kind*

New York Post

Old Marlon plays it cool all the time, now holding his head high and looking down like a Buddha, then putting his head down and looking upward and off to one side while he tries to think of what to say. It's no accident that women seem to think of him as standing at stud. . . .

The Brando, Woodward and Magnani stints are all emotionally magnificent in their highly individual ways. Maureen Stapleton and Victor Jory are also notable. There is nothing about production, performances, or direction that fails to strike one as picture making in the best, big style. Only the play itself seems questionable, though that must seem a traitorous sentiment to those who idolize Williams in all of his bizarre phases. *(Archer Winsten)*

ONE-EYED JACKS

A Paramount Pictures Release; a Pennebaker Production (1961)
Directed by Marlon Brando
Produced by Frank P. Rosenberg
Screenplay by Guy Trosper, Carlo Fiore, and Calder Willingham
Based on a novel by Charles Neider
Running time: 2 hours, 21 minutes

CAST

Rio	Marlon Brando
Dad Longworth	Karl Malden
Louisa	Pina Pellicer
Maria	Katy Jurado
Bob Amory	Ben Johnson
Lon	Slim Pickens
Modesto	Larry Duran
Harvey	Sam Gilman
Howard Tetley	Timothy Carey
Redhead	Miriam Colon
Leader of the Rurales	Rudolph Acosta
Bank Teller	Elisha Cook
Bartender	Ray Teal
Bearded Townsman	John Dierkes
Flamenco Dancer	Margarita Cordova
Doc	Hank Worden
Margarita	Nina Martinez

New York Herald Tribune

Apparently one cannot judge Brando as a director on the basis of this film as it stands. He has gone on record as dissatisfied with its present state. It ran five hours when he finished it but has been cut—not by him—to its present two hours and twenty-one minutes. Yet so much of it bears the stamp of his personality—in its visual excitement and intensity—that it still suggests that Brando, the director, has considerable promise. *(Paul V. Beckley)*

The New York Times

Marlon Brando, like young Alexander (Alexander the Great, that is), sighs for more worlds to conquer in the universe of films . . .

With Pina Pellicer, *One-Eyed Jacks*

What is extraordinary about it is that it proceeds in two contrasting styles. One is hard and realistic; the other is romantic and lush. All the way through it runs a jangle of artistic ambivalence. It is as if it had been directed jointly by John Huston and Raoul Walsh. *(Bosley Crowther)*

New York Daily News ★ ★ ★ ★

. . . It is an unusual picture of California's early settlers, who fought their gun battles not only in the mountains, but on the shores of the Pacific. The background shots reveal stunning land and seascapes, and the old town of Monterey, with its colorful Spanish-speaking population and Andalusian type of architecture, is fascinatingly re-created on the screen.

There may be differences of opinion on Brando's finished product . . . I was . . . vastly impressed with Marlon's work as producer, director and star. *(Kate Cameron)*

The New Republic

. . . Brando shows here a vigorous directorial talent . . . But this film isn't sufficiently meaty or novel to explain why Brando chose it as his first directorial-acting effort. *(Stanley Kauffmann)*

Saturday Review

The script troubles Marlon Brando is supposed to have encountered before finishing his own production, "One-Eyed Jacks," would now seem well ironed out, because the movie is a slick, professional Western, not as forthright as "High Noon," nor as evocative as "Shane," but certainly among the best of the type.

. . . Brando's performance is fierce, moody and flamboyant by turns (and is basically a series of variations on the kind of acting he unveiled as Stanley Kowalski); serving him well as a foil is the skilled Karl Malden. But the acting aside, the movie obeys most of the conventions of the Western form, complete with fast draws and the standard number of corpses. While it keeps one occupied and entertained, it is likely to take its place in movie history largely as a Western that took four years to make. *(Hollis Alpert)*

New York Post

It is doubtful that Marlon Brando has revolutionized the American Western or even rid the temple of every last cliché in "One-Eyed Jacks." . . . But as director he has given a big chance to a well-established actor, himself.

. . . Brando cannot be considered much of a trailblazer. He has chosen a most popular subject, the Western, and given it a most popular treatment.

It hardly seems necessary to praise him too, for he should make two barrels of money out of it. Still, just in case art lovers want to know, his performance is tophole, as usual, and his directing is forceful, lively and possessed of a good sense of character.

With Katy Jurado, Karl Malden, Pina Pellicer, *One-Eyed Jacks*

MUTINY ON THE BOUNTY

An M-G-M Release; an Arcola Picture Production (1962)
Directed by Lewis Milestone
Produced by Aaron Rosenberg
Screenplay by Charles Lederer
Based on the novel by Charles Nordhoff and James Norman Hall
Running time: 2 hours, 59 minutes

CAST

Fletcher Christian	Marlon Brando
Maimiti	Tarita
William Bligh	Trevor Howard
John Mills	Richard Harris
Alexander Smith	Hugh Griffith
William Brown	Richard Haydn
Edward Young	Tim Seely
Matthew Quintal	Percy Herbert
Edward Birkett	Gordon Jackson
William McCoy	Noel Purcell

New York Herald Tribune

This three-hour 1962 version of "Mutiny on the Bounty" has a raw vitality, a kind of brawling magnificence, not a little of which is due to the presence of Marlon Brando. He may be a trifle too arch for comfort occasionally or may roll his eyes at the native girls until you think he's playing a game of marbles but none the less manages to justify the camera's virtually continuous concentration on him.

He has settled on playing this newest Mr. Christian as a supercilious British gentleman who trips aboard the Bounty and presents himself with airy unconcern to Trevor Howard's Captain Bligh. My memory of Charles Laughton's Bligh is more vivid than Clark Gable's Christian in the original "Bounty," but Brando has utterly reversed matters. After the mutiny, when he is crouching in his cabin, he looks unfortunately too much like a small boy with the sulks, and the scene isn't helped much when his particular native girl, Tarita, comes in and talks about what a pigsty he's made of the place. But such moments do not dispel the general slashing vigor of his performance. *(Paul V. Beckley)*

In *Mutiny on the Bounty*

With Trevor Howard,
Mutiny on the Bounty

New York Post

. . . the picture is a big and gaudy show, built to entertain, not to stand as research.

Brando, on the other hand, and Howard, take their responsibilities more seriously. Brando comes in with an upperclass English accent that can stun an American with its eerie precision. Perhaps a Britisher could find a flaw, not this department. With these speeches Brando forever lays to rest the persistent ghost of Stanley Kowalski.

. . . The romantic interest, represented by pretty Tarita, the girl who rubs noses with Marlon Brando, is mild, running a distinct third to the Christian-Bligh thing and the gorgeous struggles with the angry sea at Cape Horn.

Unfortunately the weakest part of the picture comes at the very end where Marlon is permitted the luxury—or permits it to himself—of a lingering death cut from ancient melodrama. After three hours of blood, thunder, mountainous waves and passions boiling over, it comes a little hard to sit there patiently while Marlon strings it out.

The New York Times

There is so much in this picture that is stirring and beautiful that it is painful to note and call attention to the fact that it also has faults. But it has, and the most obvious of them is the way Marlon Brando makes Fletcher Christian an eccentric who dominates the entire dramatic scheme.

Where Trevor Howard puts wire and scrap-iron into the bulky, brutal character of Captain Bligh, making him really quite a fearful and unassailable martinet, Mr. Brando puts tinsel and cold-cream into Christian's oddly foppish frame, setting him up as more a dandy than a formidable ship's officer. When he comes aboard the vessel, he is wearing the most elaborate clothes, squiring two elegant ladies and speaking with extravagant airs. The clothes and the ladies he abandons, but he maintains the airs, to the point where one feels the performance is intended either as a travesty or a lark.

. . . Withal, Mr. Brando's steel-spring vigor when the patience of Christian snaps and he whiplashes into the fateful incitement of mutiny is truly electrifying. And his later portrayal of the shock and blanching reaction of Christian when he realizes what he has done—when he senses his fall from duty—is thoroughly reasoned and mature. *(Bosley Crowther)*

In *Mutiny on the Bounty*

THE UGLY AMERICAN

A Universal Pictures Release (1963)
Directed by George Englund
Produced by George Englund
Screenplay by Stewart Stern
Based on the novel by Eugene Burdick and William J. Lederer
Running time: 2 hours

CAST

Harrison Carter MacWhite	Marlon Brando
Deong	Eiji Okada
Marion MacWhite	Sandra Church
Homer Atkins	Pat Hingle
Grainger	Arthur Hill
Emma Atkins	Jocelyn Brando
Prime Minister Kwen Sai	Kukrit Pramoi
Joe Bing	Judson Pratt
Rachani	Reiko Sato
Munsang	George Shibata
Senator Brenner	Judson Laire
Sears	Philip Ober
Sawad	Yee Tak Yip
Andrei Krupitzyn	Stefan Schnabel
Colonel Chee	Pock Rock Ahn

The New York Times

The last time we saw Marlon Brando (in a motion picture, that is) he was dying hideously on Pitcairn Island. . . . he is back in the world of the living, entirely himself again. And whatever professional dishonor he may have suffered for his Bounty role should be wiped out by the soundness and vigor of the performance he gives in this.

. . . Brando, playing a do-goodish and determined American diplomat caught up in the conflicts of the cold war in a Southeast Asian land, comes through with an intricate and charming revelation of a decent, daring man who wants to be fair and constructive but is hobbled by his own naivete. *(Bosley Crowther)*

New York Daily News ★ ★ ★ ★

Marlon Brando gives one of his best performances in . . . "The Ugly

In *The Ugly American*

American" . . . The role of the Ambassador . . . has been made to order for Brando. He injects authority into the character of the American diplomat and projects him with clarity on the screen.

. . . I'm not sure whether the film retains the author's point of view on our diplomatic services and on our foreign policy. *(Kate Cameron)*

New York Herald Tribune

Brando rises above the naivete of his role, giving an interesting portrait of a pig-headed man of good intention, leavening it with youthful charm and good humor. . . .

In *The Ugly American*

BEDTIME STORY

A Universal Pictures Release (1964)
Directed by Ralph Levy
Produced by Stanley Shapiro
Screenplay by Shapiro and Paul Henning
Running time: 1 hour, 39 minutes

CAST

Freddy	Marlon Brando
Lawrence	David Niven
Janet	Shirley Jones
Fanny Eubank	Dody Goodman
Andre	Aram Stephan
Colonel Williams	Parley Baer
Mrs. Sutton	Marie Windsor
Miss Trumble	Rebecca Sand
Miss Harrington	Frances Robinson
Anna	Susane Cramer
Frieda	Cynthia Lynn

The New York Times

Marlon Brando is full of surprises. That's part of his stock in trade. He loves to do the unexpected and then sit back, and let his public gasp. That's what he's doing in "Bedtime Story," which came to the Palace yesterday. He is departing from his usual style completely and playing a ring-a-ding comedy character.

Not just a normal one, either—not a type patterned after Cary Grant or one of those feather-headed fellows such as those Jack Lemmon usually plays. He is acting a low-down conniver, a sweet-talking, free-wheeling fraud who will do anything to fool a woman and soften her resistance to him. And especially when he's up against a champion at fooling women on the international scene, a bogus prince played by David Niven, he's not above any dirty scheme.

Such is the flabbergasting fellow that Mr. Brando plays, and equally flabbergasting is that he gets away with it. . . . *(Bosley Crowther)*

With Shirley Jones, *Bedtime Story*

New York Herald Tribune

... Brando, who—to put it politely—is getting a bit chubby, exhibits —to put it still more politely—no particular bent for light comedy. ... *(Judith Crist)*

New York Daily News ★ ★ ½★

Marlon Brando essays a comedy role for the first time ... Brando has made a good try, but in spite of his effort to make the transition from drama to comedy he doesn't come off too well. His attempts at light comedy are pretty heavy-handed. *(Kate Cameron)*

David Niven looks on, *Bedtime Story*

THE SABOTEUR: CODE NAME—MORITURI

A 20th Century-Fox Release (1965)
Directed by Bernard Wicki
Produced by Aaron Rosenberg
Screenplay by Daniel Taradash
Based on the novel by Werner Joerg Luedecke
Running time: 2 hours, 3 minutes

CAST

Robert Crain	Marlon Brando
Captain Mueller	Yul Brynner
Esther	Janet Margolin
Colonel Statter	Trevor Howard
Kruse	Martin Benrath
Donkeyman	Hans Christian Blech
Dr. Ambach	Wally Cox
Branner	Max Haufler
Milkereit	Rainer Penkert
Baldwin	William Redfield
Admiral	Oscar Bereal
Nissen	Martin Brandt
Ensign Sloan	Gary Crosby

New York Herald Tribune

. . . an old-fashioned war-time melodrama made tedious and pretentious by muddle-headed moralities and fuzzy latter-day cynicisms about World War II. The only noteworthy element is Marlon Brando who once again manages, amid the morass of ludicrous dialect, stilted dialogue and inane situations, to emerge as a fascinating performer . . . (*Judith Crist*)

The New York Times

So long as Marlon Brando has to play a straight melodramatic role (and that seems to be about the only sort the Hollywood people can now turn up for him), we couldn't ask to see him in one much more congenial to his style than the one he plays in the film which now goes by the turgid title of "The Saboteur: Code Name—Morituri."

. . . And he plays it with evident enjoyment, milking the moments of suspense with all his beautiful skill at holding pauses and letting tense thought churn behind his bland eyes. Again he speaks with a

In *Morituri*

With Yul Brynner, *Morituri*

juicy German accent, as he did in "The Young Lions," and affects the elegant air of a fellow who packs an iron fist in a silken glove . . . *(Bosley Crowther)*

New York Post

. . . There are three sources of spectator fun: 1) Brando as a German is splendid in attitude, marvelous in accent . . . *(Archer Winsten)*

New York Daily News

. . . There are several effective performances, including . . . Brando . . . *(Kate Cameron)*

THE CHASE

A Columbia Pictures Release (1966)
Directed by Arthur Penn
Produced by Sam Spiegel
Screenplay by Lillian Hellman
Based on a novel and play by Horton Foote
Running time: 2 hours, 15 minutes

CAST

Calder	Marlon Brando
Anna	Jane Fonda
Bubber	Robert Redford
Val Rogers	E. G. Marshall
Ruby	Angie Dickinson
Emily Stewart	Janice Rule
Mrs. Reeves	Miriam Hopkins
Mary Fuller	Martha Hyer
Edwin Stewart	Robert Duvall
Briggs	Henry Hull
Elizabeth Rogers	Diana Hyland
Jason Rogers	James Fox
Mrs. Briggs	Jocelyn Brando
Damon Fuller	Richard Bradford
Verna Dee	Katherine Walsh

The New York Times

. . . outrageously clumsy an attempt to blend a weak but conceivably dramatic theme of civil rights with a whole mess of small-town misbehaviors of the sort that you get in "Peyton Place." It appears a deliberate endeavor to mix the message of "High Noon" and sex.

. . . To be sure, the character assigned [Brando] is ambiguous and gross, and Mr. Brando cannot make it any more than a stubborn, growling cop. . . .

. . . Yes, it's a phony, tasteless movie. . . .

New York Daily News ★ ★ ½★

. . . The characters are cardboard setups to be knocked down by the continual sniping of the authors.

In *The Chase*

In *The Chase*

. . . Marlon Brando plays the sheriff in a low key, but gives some authority to the role. *(Kate Cameron)*

New York Herald Tribune

"The Chase" is contrivance from beginning to end—a successful contrivance. . . .

. . . Marlon Brando is a Marlon Brando sheriff, terse and true and stolid, even when beaten to a gloriously bloody near-pulp. . . . *(Judith Crist)*

THE APPALOOSA

A Universal Pictures Release (1966)
Directed by Sidney J. Furie
Produced by Alan Miller
Screenplay by James Bridges and Roland Kibbee
Based on a novel by Robert MacLeod
Running time: 1 hour, 39 minutes

CAST

Matt	Marlon Brando
Trini	Anjanette Comer
Chuy	John Saxon
Lazaro	Emilio Fernandez
Squint-Eye	Alex Montoya
Ana	Miriam Colon
Paco	Rafael Compos
Ramos	Frank Silvera

New York Daily News ★ ★ ★

. . . The ill-fitting vehicle would have accomplished just as much for any nondescript actor who could fake a Mexican accent and darken his skin with coffee beans. . . . *(Kathleen Carroll)*

The New York Times

An odd sort of Western movie. . . .
To be quite blunt about it, it is on the bold, pretentious side. . . .
Mr. Brando and Mr. Saxon are sullen and sinewy in their roles. . . .
(Bosley Crowther)

New York World Journal-Tribune

. . . If we're to go in for the perennial alibi that Marlon Brando hadn't material worthy of his talents, we must congratulate him on keeping a straight face—and he does, throughout. At least he sounds like Brando. . . . *(Judith Crist)*

Variety

. . . Brando delivers a rambling performance, occasionally managing a dynamic enactment of the man. . . . *('Whit')*

Time

... In a role that a lesser actor might easily saunter through, Brando handicaps himself with a fiercely concentrated acting style more suitable for great occasions. He seems determined to play not just a man but a whole concept of humanity. ...

In *The Appaloosa*

A COUNTESS FROM HONG KONG

A Universal Pictures Release (1967)
Directed by Charles Chaplin
Produced by Jerome Epstein
Screenplay by Charles Chaplin
Running time: 1 hour, 48 minutes

CAST

Ogden	Marlon Brando
Natascha	Sophia Loren
Harvey	Sydney Chaplin
Martha	Tippi Hedren
Hudson	Patrick Cargill
Miss Gaulswallow	Margaret Rutherford
John Felix	Michael Medwin
Clark	Oliver Johnston
Captain	John Paul
Society Girl	Angela Scoular
Steward	Peter Barlett
Crawford	Bill Nagy
Old Steward	Charles Chaplin

The New York Times

. . . [Chaplin] failed to surround his story with a sufficiently clever slapstick style, and he certainly failed to communicate his intention to Mr. Brando and Miss Loren. They march and sashay through this burietta about an American ambassador who is put to the embarrassing inconvenience of having to conceal a stowaway Russian countess in his suite aboard a Pacific-crossing ship as though they were in high comedy by Freddie Lonsdale or Noel Coward, trying to be elegant and airy, with ditch-water dull dialogue. *(Bosley Crowther)*

New York Daily News ★ ★ ½★

. . . a fairy tale so hopelessly out of date that, remembering the Chaplin genius, it is almost pathetic.

Had Chaplin been Ross Hunter one might have forgiven him. . . .

. . . Brando is like a bull in a china shop when it comes to comedy. His brows knit together, his mouth drooping in his "gas pain" expression, Brando broods and Miss Loren understandably freezes at the sight. *(Kathleen Carroll)*

With Charles Chaplin, *A Countess from Hong Kong*

The New Yorker

. . . Marlon Brando and Sophia Loren are made to suffer innumerable professional indignities under his direction. These days, Mr. Brando often gives the impression of being revolted by having to work in movies at all; in this picture his revulsion nearly succeeds in bringing a silly character to life by killing it. *(Brendan Gill)*

In *A Countess from Hong Kong*

REFLECTIONS IN A GOLDEN EYE

A Warner Brothers-Seven Arts Release (1967)
Directed by John Huston
Produced by Ray Stark
Screenplay by Chapman Mortimer and Gladys Hill
Based on the novel by Carson McCullers
Running time: 1 hour, 49 minutes

CAST

Leonora Penderton	Elizabeth Taylor
Maj. Weldon Penderton	Marlon Brando
Lieut. Col. Morris Langdon	Brian Keith
Alison Langdon	Julie Harris
Private Williams	Robert Forster
Anacleto	Zorro David
Stables Sergeant	Gordon Mitchell
Captain Weincheck	Irvin Dugan
Susie	Fay Sparks

The New York Times

Hell hath no homicidal fury like a homosexual scorned. . . .

Some characters are more interesting than others. The one Mr. Brando plays is basically most important, but his fascination fluctuates with the actor's performance of the role. At times he is devastating, as he sullenly and painfully reveals the helplessness and self-knowledge of a would-be he-man who is not. *(Bosley Crowther)*

New York Post

. . . the performances are such that you just can't laugh at it. Brando has never been greater. His solitary frenzy of fear, relief and anger, brought about by a horse running away with him, is awesome in its approach to insanity. *(Archer Winsten)*

New York Daily News ★ ★ ½★

"Reflections" Just Dull and Dirty . . .

Considering the stars . . . and the director, John Huston, it is unfortunate that the efforts of this amalgamated talent result unfavorably.

. . . Marlon Brando, whose face is expressionless in an unearthly glow. He looks as if he should be on exhibition at Madame Tussaud's in London. *(Wanda Hale)*

In *Reflections
in a Golden Eye*

With Elizabeth Taylor, *Reflections in a Golden Eye*

CANDY

A Cinerama Releasing Corporation Release (1968)
Directed by Christian Marquand
Produced by Robert Haggiag
Screenplay by Buck Henry
Based on the novel by Terry Southern
Running time: 1 hour, 59 minutes

CAST

Candy	Ewa Aulin
The Hunchback	Charles Aznavour
Grindl	Marlon Brando
McPhisto	Richard Burton
Dr. Krankeit	James Coburn
Dr. Dunlap	John Huston
General Smight	Walter Matthau
Emmanuel	Ringo Starr
Daddy and Uncle Jack	John Astin
Livia	Elsa Martinelli
Zero	Sugar Ray Robinson

New York Daily News ★ ★

. . . It is in reality just a dirty movie. In fact, it is, as of this very moment, the ultimate dirty movie. . . . *(Kathleen Carroll)*

The New York Times

The movie, directed by Christian Marquand, manages to compromise, by its relentless, crawling, bloody lack of talent, almost anyone who had anything to do with it. Richard Burton, as a poet-seducer, gives a firm, delighted, irrefutable demonstration of his lack of any comic talent whatsoever. John Huston and Ringo Starr look as though they had been drawn in by a regrettable, humorless beautiful people syndrome. Charles Aznavour performs uncrisply and badly as the hunchback. Marlon Brando, as a Jewish guru (the film has an ugly racialism and arrested development, frog-torturing soft sadism at its heart), is less unendurable, because one is glad to see him on the screen in anything again. . . . *(Renata Adler)*

New York Post

The fourth, final and devastating sequence finds Marlon Brando as Guru Grindl. He sets out to teach Candy other ways of breathing, not merely the customary in and out. It is possible that you will not ever again be able to view an Indian Guru without seeing Marlon Brando as he approaches ocular ecstacy and tries to get his Lotus position-entangled legs loose. *(Archer Winsten)*

With Ewa Aulin, *Candy*

THE NIGHT OF THE FOLLOWING DAY

A Universal Pictures Release (1969)
Produced and directed by Hubert Cornfield
Screenplay by Hubert Cornfield
Based on the novel by Lionel White
Running time: 1 hour, 33 minutes

CAST

Chauffeur	Marlon Brando
Leer	Richard Boone
The Blonde	Rita Moreno
The Girl	Pamela Franklin
Friendly	Jess Hahn
Fisherman/cop	Gerard Buhr
Father	Hughes Wanner
Bartender	Jacques Marin

New York Daily News

Brando, slimmed down, never looked better and he is back in his old relaxed style of playing a role, saying his words clearly, as if he were the first to think of them. And he has the best lines. *(Wanda Hale)*

The New York Times

It's high time that Marlon Brando landed himself a good picture, but "The Night of the Following Day" is emphatically not the one.

. . . Say this for Mr. Brando. Trimmed down, he looks better than he has in years . . . *(Howard Thompson)*

The New Yorker

. . . in two of the cardboard-cutout roles he cast Marlon Brando and Richard Boone—actors who have such phenomenal audience rapport that the audience is *with* them even when they're doing nothing, and doing that badly. I don't think Brando has ever been worse or less interesting than in this movie—not even in "A Countess from Hong Kong"—yet Brando is, after all, our great *original*. And the audience is so drawn to his singularity that it seems happy just to watch him do some dumb little thing, like stare at his girl when she's all doped up and pretending not to be . . . But though probably almost no one accepts Brando and Boone in their roles, their very presence evokes a

With Rita Moreno, *The Night of the Following Day*

special empathy—not simply because they're stars but because their edge of irony about what they're doing and their uncertainty about how to play the comic-strip gangsters makes the difference for the audience between just laughing at the picture and laughing both ways. *(Pauline Kael)*

BURN!

A United Artists Corporation Release (1970)
Directed by Gillo Pontecorvo
Produced by Alberto Grimaldi
Screenplay by Franco Solinas and Giorgio Artorio
Based on an original story by Mr. Pontecorvo, Mr. Solinas and Mr. Artorio
Running time: 1 hour, 52 minutes

CAST

Sir William Walker	Marlon Brando
Jose Dolores	Everisto Marquez
Teddy Sanchez	Renato Salvatori
Shelton	Norman Hill
General Prada	Tom Lyons
Guarina	Wanani

The New York Times

"Burn!," Gillo Pontecorvo's first film since "The Battle of Algiers," aspires to be a prole epic but winds up as the sort of prole pageant in which characters always seem to be conceptualizing great issues, mostly freedom, as they pass in front of history, as if it were a scenic view, instead of moving in and out of it.

. . . "Burn!" . . . can't be dominated by . . . the British agent, whom Mr. Brando plays with a marvelously complex, rueful intelligence. . . .

In the course of its production, "Burn!" . . . turned into a kind of mini "Cleopatra." . . .

. . . I must add that I wasn't bored by the film for a minute. . . . Mr. Brando is worth watching under almost any circumstances, and you should enjoy seeing him here, using that Fletcher Christian accent and, towards the end of the film, looking very much like the late Ernest Hemingway, a tired and tragic hero whom life has somehow double-crossed. . . . *(Vincent Canby)*

Time

After the debacle of "Mutiny on the Bounty," Brando should have known enough to stay away from tropical adventurism and English accents. He shows vestiges of genius, but his artistry is subordinated to Pontecorvo's ambition. . . . *(Mark Goodman)*

With director Pontecorvo, *Burn!*

In *Burn!*

New York Post

It offers Brando doing his Britisher imitation, a very nice thing it is, too. . . .

Unfortunately, Pontecorvo's brilliant re-enactments of "Algiers" don't work as well for "Burn." . . . *(Archer Winsten)*

THE NIGHTCOMERS

An Avco-Embassy Release: a Kastner-Ladd-Kanter presentation of a Scimitar (Michael Winner) Production. (1972)
Directed by Michael Winner
Screenplay by Michael Hastings
Running time: 1 hour, 36 minutes

CAST

Quint	Marlon Brando
Miss Jessel	Stephanie Beacham
Mrs. Grose	Tora Hird
Flora	Verna Harvey
Miles	Christopher Ellis
Tutor	Harry Andrews
Governess	Anna Palk

New York Daily News

. . . Marlon Brando, given a story of consequence, a tactful director and a role he can come alive in, will get a firmer grip on his followers of long standing who've seen him through some mediocre shows.

Such is the case in "The Nightcomers." . . .

. . . All roles are played beautifully but "The Nightcomers" is Marlon's picture.

The American star gives an uncanny interpretation of Peter Quint, Irish gardener, unkempt and crude, who forces his passion on the genteel governess. But he is gentle with orphaned children. . . . *(Wanda Hale)*

Daily News

. . . a movie that finally gives Marlon Brando his finest acting role in years. . . .

Brando is simply riveting as the eccentric, degenerate Quint, slimed up to resemble a muddy potato that talks like Barry Fitzgerald. He really works in this movie, and the movie deserves him. *(Rex Reed)*

New York Post

"The Nightcomers" . . . proves conclusively that Marlon Brando can still take a palm as all-around character actor. . . .

. . . A special note must be given Brando whose brooding, fun-

In *The Nightcomers*

loving, cruel and sadistic Peter Quint has the lilt of Ireland in it and a lot of the black moodiness too. (*Archer Winsten*)

Time

. . . and Brando, 20 years on from Stanley Kowalski, still has the presence to make bullying cruelty captivating. (*Timothy Foote*)

With Stephanie Beacham, *The Nightcomers*

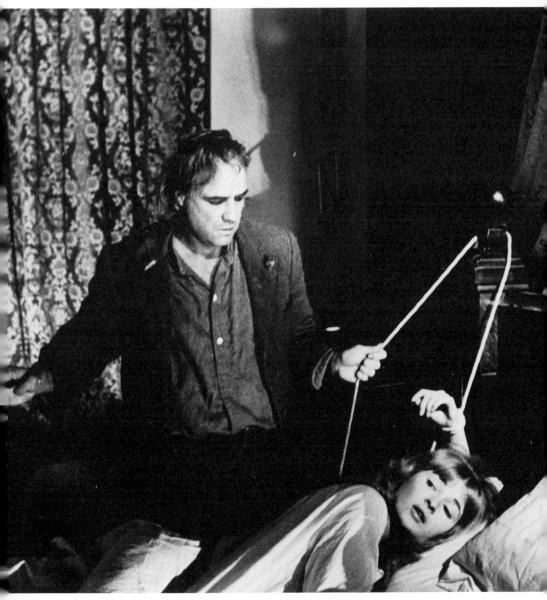

THE GODFATHER

A Paramount Pictures Release (1972)
Directed by Francis Ford Coppola
Produced by Albert S. Ruddy
Screenplay by Mario Puzo and Mr. Coppola
Based on the novel by Mr. Puzo
Running time: 2 hours, 55 minutes

CAST

Don Vito Corleone	Marlon Brando
Michael Corleone	Al Pacino
Sonny Corleone	James Caan
Clemenza	Richard Castallano
Tom Hagen	Robert Duvall
McCluskey	Sterling Hayden
Jack Woltz	John Marley
Barzini	Richard Conte
Kay Adams	Diana Keaton
Sollozzo	Al Lettieri
Tessio	Abe Vigoda
Connie Rizzi	Talia Shire
Carlo Rizzi	Gianni Russo
Fredo Corleone	John Cazale
Cuneo	Rudy Bond
Johnny Fontane	Al Martino
Mama Corleone	Morgana King

The New York Times

The film is affecting for many reasons, including the return of Marlon Brando, who has been away only in spirit, as Don Vito Corleone, the magnificent, shrewd, old Corleone patriarch. It's not a large role, but he is the key to the film, and to the contributions of all of the other performers. . . . *(Vincent Canby)*

New York Daily News ★ ★ ★ ★

Marlon Brando's old flame that has glowed for years, and flickered along a trail bumpy with mediocre pictures, shines higher and brighter than ever. The old irresistible magic is revived in Paramount's "The Godfather" in his intuitive grasp of Mario Puzo's Don Corleone, a living symbol of the poetic translation of his name, the lionhearted.

In *The Godfather*

Brando is cool as the godfather, sagacious head of the Corleone "family," most powerful of the five "families" of organized crime in New York. He is relaxed as the loving, indulgent patriarch of his large blood family, in his mansion behind an iron fence in Long Beach, L. I. And he is terrifically appealing as the man who cheats death, recovers from bullet wounds inflicted by a rival gang, recuperates at home to enjoy his garden and grandchildren until he dies of old age. Once he comes out of seclusion to warn chiefs of the five "families" that the gang war must stop.

Brando is the strong magnet that will draw fans to "The Godfather." . . . (Wanda Hale)

With Al Pacino, *The Godfather*

Original drawing of
Brando as *The Godfather*

New York Post

The Brando performance as Don Corleone is the cornerstone. He's squat, his prognathous jaw signals his will, his thoughtful brow indicates the reason behind his moves. The measure of this performance is the way you think of him as Don Corleone, not Brando. *(Archer Winsten)*

The New Yorker

The enormous cast is headed by Marlon Brando as Don Vito Corleone, the "godfather" of a powerful Sicilian-American clan, with James Caan as his hothead son, Sonny, and Al Pacino as the thoughtful, educated son Michael. Is Brando marvellous? Yes, he is, but then he often is; he was marvellous a few years ago in "Reflections in a Golden Eye," and he's shockingly effective as a working-class sadist in a current film, "The Nightcomers," though the film itself isn't worth seeing. The role of Don Vito—a patriarch in his early sixties—allows him to release more of the gentleness that was so seductive and unsettling in his braggart roles. Don Vito could be played as a magnificent old warrior, a noble killer, a handsome bull-patriarch, but Brando manages to debanalize him. It's typical of Brando's daring that he doesn't capitalize on his broken-prow profile and the massive, sculptural head that has become the head of Rodin's Balzac—he doesn't play for statuesque nobility. The light, cracked voice comes out of a twisted mouth and clenched teeth; he has the battered face of a devious, combative old man, and a pugnacious thrust to his jaw. The rasp in his voice is particularly effective after Don Vito has been wounded; one almost feels that the bullets cracked it, and wishes it hadn't been cracked before. Brando interiorizes Don Vito's power, makes him less physically threatening and *deeper*, hidden within himself. *(Pauline Kael)*

LAST TANGO IN PARIS
(ULTIMO TANGO A PARIGI)

A United Artists Release; a P.E.A.–Artistes Associés Production (1972)
Directed by Bernardo Bertolucci
Produced by Alberto Grimaldi
Script by Mr. Bertolucci and Franco Arcalli
Running time: 2 hours, 10 minutes

CAST

Paul	Marlon Brando
Jeanne	Maria Schneider
Concierge	Darling Legitmus
Tom	Jean-Pierre Léaud
TV script girl	Catherine Sola
TV cameraman	Mauro Marchetti
TV sound engineer	Dan Diament
TV asst. cameraman	Peter Schommer
Catherine	Catherine Allegret
Monique	Marie-Helen Breillat
Mouchette	Catherine Breillat
Marcel	Massimo Girotti
Barge Captain	Jean Luc Bideau
Miss Blandish	Laura Betti
Prostitute	Giovanna Galetti
Rosa's Mother	Maria Michi

The New York Times

The feelings of love, anguish and despair that erupt all over the place in Bernardo Bertolucci's new film, "Last Tango in Paris," are so intense, so consuming, that watching the film at times comes close to being an embarrassment. . . .

"Last Tango in Paris" is all about romantic love, but its expressions are the sometimes brave, sometimes wildly foolish-looking Lawrentian gestures of an intense sexual passion that goes as far as it can and then collapses in physical and emotional exhaustion. . . .

The film is about Paul (Marlon Brando), a middle-aged American of obscure antecedents who has been living in Paris for seven years with his wife, the beautiful patronne of a second-rate hotel. When the film opens, the wife has just committed suicide and Paul is coolly setting up

With Maria Schneider, *Last Tango in Paris*

With Maria Schneider, *Last Tango in Paris*

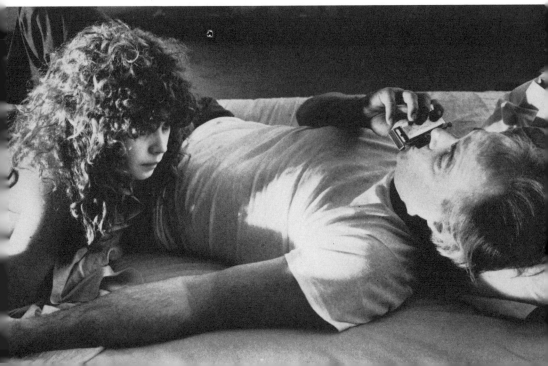

an apartment with a girl whose name he does not want to know, whose feelings he does not want to hear, for afternoons of pure, absolutely free sexual encounters.

. . . Brando, like Bertolucci, has pulled out all the stops without fear of looking absurd. . . . *(Vincent Canby)*

Variety

Bernardo Bertolucci's "Last Tango in Paris" . . . emerges . . . as an uneven, convoluted, certainly dispute-provoking study of sexual passion in which Marlon Brando gives a truly remarkable performance. . . .

For Brando it serves as a showcase for a brave and bravura performance, a stunning portrait of one of life's casualties, rich in pathos, self-disgust, and surprising humor. This is no mannered walk-through, nor does it smack of "performance" as did his much-praised "God-father" stint. Working in French and English, some of it apparently improvisational, Brando holds nothing back. It's one of the riskiest acting jobs ever undertaken by a major film talent, and to Brando's credit it is never embarrassing. *('Verr')*

The New Yorker

The movie breakthrough has finally come. Exploitation films have been supplying mechanized sex—sex as physical stimulant but without any passion or emotional violence. The sex in "Last Tango in Paris" expresses the characters' drives. . . .

Realism with the terror of actual experience still alive on the screen —that's what Bertolucci and Brando achieve . . . Bertolucci builds a structure that supports improvisation. Everything is prepared, but everything is subject to change, and the whole film is alive with a sense of discovery. Bertolucci builds the characters "on what the actors are in themselves. I never ask them to interpret something preexistent, except for dialogue—and even that changes a lot." For Bertolucci, the actors "make the characters." And Brando knows how to improvise: it isn't just Brando improvising, it's Brando improvising as Paul . . . When Brando improvises with Bertolucci's structure, his full art is realized. . . .

. . . Expressing a character's sexuality makes new demands on an actor, and Brando has no trick accent to play with this time, and no putty on his face. It's perfectly apparent that the role was conceived for Brando, using elements of his past as integral parts of the character . . . The excitement of Brando's performance here is in the revelation of how creative screen acting can be. At the simplest level, Brando, by his inflections and rhythms, the right American obscenities, and perhaps an improvised monologue, makes Paul an authentic American abroad, in a way that an Italian writer-director simply couldn't do without the actor's help. At a more complex level, he helps Bertolucci discover the movie in the process of shooting it, and that's what makes moviemaking an art. *(Pauline Kael)*

238

With Maria Schneider, *Last Tango in Paris*

INDEX